THE TRUTH ABOUT ANGELS

In memory of astronaut Edgar Mitchell and all who seek true and deep meaning.

THE TRUTH ABOUT ANGELS

DECODING THE SECRET WORLD AND LANGUAGE OF THE AFTERLIFE

THERESA CHEUNG

First published in Great Britain in 2021 by Yellow Kite
An imprint of Hodder & Stoughton
An Hachette UK company

3

A CIP catalogue record for this title is available from the British Library

Trade Paperback ISBN 978 1 529 34142 3
eBook ISBN 978 1 529 34143 0

Typeset in Sabon MT by Hewer Text UK Ltd, Edinburgh
Printed and bound in Great Britain by Clays Ltd, Elcograf S.p.A.

Hodder & Stoughton policy is to use papers that are natural, renewable and recyclable products and made from wood grown in sustainable forests. The logging and manufacturing processes are expected to conform to the environmental regulations of the country of origin.

Yellow Kite
Hodder & Stoughton Ltd
Carmelite House
50 Victoria Embankment
London EC4Y 0DZ

www.yellowkitebooks.co.uk

CONTENTS

'Three things cannot be long hidden:
the sun, the moon and the truth.'

BUDDHA

FOREWORD

Talk to the Heart

It is often said that the truth shall set you free. And the place to find said truth is in the heart. So, if your heart could talk to you, reveal its truth, right here, right now in these troubled times when truth no longer feels sacred, what would it say?

I believe it would talk about the only truth it knows, which is that unseen force called love. It would whisper fond memories and share other invisible but real sensations, mixing all that exists beyond the material into a message of eternal truth.

Your heart would not try to hide or spin its only truth but speak with pride of its many scars – all those times it has been shattered yet re-formed into something stronger and greater. It would hum gently about the wonder of hope or the transformative feelings of joy and connection you experience with loved ones or when immersed in nature or doing what you love. Your heart would sing about living on purpose and with integrity and your desire to do the right thing, be kinder to yourself and others. It would share comforting tales of intuition, dreams and coincidences inspiring you, alongside enchanting messages of empathy, creativity, gratitude and laughter.

And the miracle is that it could express all of this to you by uttering just one word – a word that encapsulates everything true your heart has ever wanted to say to you – 'angels'.

If your heart could talk it would speak to you for ever about angels – the angels living within and all around you. It would long for you to let your angels guide you. It would urge you to see, hear and feel your angels because in every heartbeat, they are speaking to you loud and clear. It would love you to know that once you start listening clearly to your angels in this way, there's absolutely no going back. Your life can never feel or be the same again.

You may not yet know your angels, let alone trust them, believe you deserve them or be able to recognise their voices. But it is precisely when you feel all hope and connection to something higher and greater than yourself is lost that unseen guidance from above and within can break through with calm certainty. As you read or listen, reflect on your life and tune into the beating of your own heart. Know that your angels are not just calling out to you and letting you know they are there – they are also listening intently, right here, right now. They long to hear you speak their truth, which is your only truth. No more excuses: isn't it high time you started that honest conversation?

INTRODUCTION

Where Have All the Angels Gone?

Increasing numbers of people are feeling empty, doing what is expected of them – whether that be chasing career, relationships, wealth, status – but reaching a point of no return, when all that material 'stuff' isn't enough any more. They want deeper purpose. The 2020 pandemic, and the chaos, division and grief it has left in its wake, has only heightened further this craving, this deep longing for more meaning.

SILENT NO MORE

Whenever you start to wonder if there is something more or a purpose or meaning to your life, it is because angels are calling your name. It's a potentially transformative moment of self-awareness. But it's also a moment when you may feel directionless, so seek guidance from the wealth of teachings out there.

Chances are, if you love the idea of angels looking out for you, you are a sensitive soul. You believe what others say easily. You may be eager to please. If you get anything at all out of this book, I hope it will be the knowledge and understanding that you can – must – always ask questions, believe what others *do*, not just what they say, and listen to what *your* intuition tells you rather than being swayed by the expectations of others. In other words, I hope you will grow your own wings.

If you are feeling vulnerable – and so many of us are right now, with the world reeling from the pandemic – it is so easy to trust without questioning, especially in terms of ideas and words such as 'love', 'light' and 'angels'. In the pages that follow you are repeatedly going to be encouraged to ask challenging questions of yourself and everything you think you know or have ever been led to believe about angels. In the process you will find the curiosity and the courage you need to discover the truth about them; the truth that can feed your heart and soul and set you free.

SETTING YOU FREE

I hope the honesty of this book washes away any misinformation and unhelpful ideas you may have heard and read about angels. And I hope that, at the same time, it might just prove to you in a new way that angels are real – pure and simple.

Of course, it's hard to prove that angels exist. Proof is very much of the material world, whereas angels belong to feelings, intuition, dreams and an unseen world that operates in ways our rational minds can't yet understand. So here I'm not just going to rely on anecdotal evidence, my personal experience or ancient teachings and wisdom. For the last few years, I have been collaborating with scientists researching the paranormal. Science searches for the truth through facts and it is the science of angels that I entreat you to put your trust in now. This emerging science of consciousness has so far been largely hidden in scientific journals and complicated by jargon. My mission has been to make the science accessible, mainstream.

Of course, your personal beliefs concerning angels will come into it. If you are reading this book, the chances are you are inclined to believe in angels. But I implore you to read with your sceptical hat on. Listen, but ask questions. Don't accept everything you are told. Questions are infinitely more powerful than answers when it comes to spiritual and personal growth. Questions encourage you to learn, seek out new horizons and focus on what you feel and think rather than what is handed down. Once something becomes known or answered, the learning stops. Curiosity – willingness to learn – is what gives your life direction.

I'm certainly not asking you to believe what I believe whenever I offer my opinion. There's a huge and important difference between opinion and fact and I want to make that clear from the start. I have always encouraged people not to follow or copy me but to just let the information I share open their minds, encourage debate. I'm simply asking you to review the evidence I will present, flex your empathy muscle (that is, understand even if you don't agree with the perspective offered) and keep an open mind. Remember, it is when minds close that life stagnates and all hope of discovering any truth or meaning is lost.

Modern scientists are themselves open-minded; they are increasingly willing to take the power of belief and subjective experience into consideration in their research and to admit there are some things about this life they don't (yet) understand. I'll explore this amazing development later in the book.

The personal stories of people who believe in angels and the afterlife are comforting and mesmerising, and remind us that there is more to this life than meets the eye. They serve an important role. But this book walks a path less travelled. It encourages a more questioning approach to paranormal experiences and insights. At the risk of repeating myself, the meaning of life is discovered not through unquestioning acceptance of what others tell you is the 'truth' or by remaining the same, but through curiosity and embracing the transformative wisdom of change.

Your angels would have it no other way.

EYES WIDE SHUT

I'm inviting you to think about angels in the same way you think about your night-time dreams. If you dream – which is the same as saying 'if you breathe' because everyone dreams – you are already comprehending the truth about angels.

Even if you don't recall doing so, research has proven that you are still dreaming. You just don't always remember. Or perhaps you do remember fragments of dreams, but because they don't make any logical sense you assume what you experienced with your eyes closed is meaningless. Like dreams, angels happen; even if you don't think they are there, they are. You just need to notice them and learn how to decode the messages they are constantly sending you.

In other words, the most authentic way to tune into the invisible world is to discover your own angels and interpreting your dreams creates awareness of your mystic potential.

It was the clear vision that 2020 brought with it that made me look at spirituality as it is being presented today in a radically new light. There is much talk of spirit guides, angel realms, affirmations, ascension, intentions . . . but this all just distracts from the simple truth about angels – which is that they need to be discovered from the inside out.

Connection to angels simply can't be bought, or facilitated by someone else. It's got to come from *you*. Anyone who tells you otherwise is preventing you from discovering your own spellbinding truth.

In the spirit of truth that inspired this book, I suggest here (and mention again throughout) things to be aware of if you strongly feel you need to visit a lightworker, sign up to a course or treatment or buy a product. I also offer my suggestions and hopes for a better-regulated future. I'm not completely against seeking out teachers to introduce you to new ways of thinking – far from it, in fact. Learning from born teachers – wise people – is an important part of the spiritual path. But I want you to spend more time thinking about the credentials of those teachers and whether or not they are encouraging you to find your own truth about angels. The aim of the true teacher is always to make their role redundant; to help you leave the nest, spread your wings and fly.

Above all else this book is a call for you to focus on discovering within *yourself* your own ability to access truth and love, not limited by space and time. It's an encouragement not to seek validation from others or outside yourself; because truth can no more be found in that way than through relationships, career, money, status and all that material 'stuff'. The only way to find truth is from the inside out. And the ways you choose to access and express your inner truth can be seen as 'seeing angels'. These ways have similarities with the ways in which others experience their angels, because we are all connected – but they are also uniquely your own.

You are a unique miracle of DNA. There has never been anyone like you before and there never will be anyone like you again. Your angels know that. Time now for you to understand and celebrate that astonishing truth.

ANGELS FOR ME

Here's my belief about angels. Some of what I say may resonate with you; but if it doesn't, that's perfectly fine. As I have said, I want this book to ignite *your* desire to seek *your own* understanding, *your own* truth about angels. If there is an afterlife, I'm convinced that when you get there you won't be asked how much you followed or copied someone else, however worthy of following or 'gifted' or amazing that person was. You will be asked how true you were to yourself, your own truth, the best version of you. In this light the only person you should ever compare yourself to is the person you were yesterday, and the only person you should aspire to be is the better person you can be tomorrow.

I'm aware that what you have read so far is not perhaps what you would have expected to read in an 'angel' book. That's because I want to be upfront from the start about what you can expect. But let me also reassure you that although I ask some very searching questions throughout this book (how else can truth be discovered?), *I still believe in angels*.

I am convinced angels watch over my life in countless unseen ways. I believe they exist not just around me but within me. Whenever I feel a surge of sudden inspiration, compassion and love, I believe an angel is holding my heart. I know they speak loud and clear to me through my dreams and intuitions. And sometimes they call my name through the kind words or actions of others, the voices of nature or reassuring signs appearing at exactly the right time to bring me hope.

But there have also been many instances when I have seriously doubted. Typically, this doubt arises during times of deep personal despair. I'm sure I'm not alone when I say that it is far easier to believe in angels when all is right in your world, but extremely challenging when there is pain.

But doubt also arises within me as a natural reaction to the feelings of helplessness that senseless world events, natural and man-made disasters, can ignite. If your heart is hurting right now, you are certainly not alone. Collectively our hearts are bruised not just by the pandemic and other events in the material world, but also by the seemingly relentless onslaught of materialism, corruption and narcissism that has been a theme in recent decades. Part of me wonders why our angels don't simply show themselves or intervene. Sort out this mess.

I typically find myself resorting to tried-and-tested metaphors whenever people message me with their moving stories of grief and loss, asking the big 'why me?' question. I talk to them about the darkness before the dawn, the labour pains before birth, or how this life is like the underside of a tapestry – all knots and loose ends, but then you finally get to see the topside, where all makes perfect sense, in spirit or the afterlife. I'm well aware that as poetic as these beautiful metaphors are, they are often just not enough when life sucks. What we really need in times of crisis is the convincing and reassuring touch of an angel or, better still, 'proof' that they are real.

This book cannot walk the same trusting path as some of my previous books. As comforting as that might be, right now it would feel ineffective, out of tune with reality and naïve. Yes, I want this book to offer comfort. But I also want it to encourage believers to look deep within themselves and question their understanding of angels, as well as offering sceptics serious pause for thought. I want to talk about angels to the unconverted as well as the converted, and to people of all ages, cultures, beliefs and walks of life, including a younger generation tasked as they are with creating a kinder world.

I hope this book becomes a spiritual talking point that opens hearts and minds for many years to come. It's time for gentle souls who believe in the unseen power of love to find their voices and stand up for their truth. I hope it redefines your thinking about angels in an empowering way. But more than that, I'd love it to become a source of invisible reassurance for you that the truth is both within you and out there and that it is more than a match for darkness, especially if you are experiencing your dark night of the soul, have suffered a bereavement or other loss, or are simply looking for hope in an overwhelming world.

* * *

I have never claimed to know all the answers, but I do know that the only clear way out of grief and pain – whether that pain is personal or collective – is to discover a spiritual perspective; an understanding that there is more to this life than the material. This perspective then becomes your rock. It takes you to a place where you can feel connected to departed loved ones with a smile before a tear, see the bigger picture and find deeper meaning in both personal struggles and global crises. It is finding deep peace by seeing the extraordinary in the everyday. It is understanding what truth really is by focusing on the power of empathy, compassion and kindness and the invisible forces that connect rather than divide us.

It is focusing on what truly matters, finding your angels within and all around you when life feels directionless. Indeed, instead of driving you away from your angels, crisis can often be an opportunity to drive you right back into their loving arms. Take the 2020 lockdown, for example.

Throughout 2020, especially during the pandemic lockdowns, messages and questions about angels just kept on flooding in. The catalyst for this sudden interest was the simple fact that increasing numbers of people were reporting more vivid and frequent dreams.

This lockdown dream phenomenon did not surprise me at all. In my opinion, angels were choosing dreams as the most effective medium to open our minds to the reality of an unseen dimension.

As suggested earlier, dreams are the perfect way for angels to reach out to us – not only because they are subtle and unlikely to cause alarm but also because we *all* dream, whatever our belief, culture or age. Dreams connect us. They illustrate our shared humanity. The increase in our awareness of our dreams during lockdown was our angels sending us a powerful message about an urgent need to focus on what connects rather than divides us. We all need to look out for each other right now, see the suffering of others as our own, regardless of their race, culture and background.

But it's not just through your dreams that angels reach out. They are also constantly speaking to you in countless other ordinary yet extraordinary ways. You simply need to start paying attention to them, and to learn their secret language.

Through whatever medium angels call out to you, their aim is always the same – to lead you gently away from the material or basing your self-worth on externals, towards the spiritual and your infinite potential for peace and purpose there.

ANGELS CAN

Angels are sometimes thought of as a New or Now Age trend, but they have always been with us and always will be. The human race has 'mastered' the Earth, but we are also destroying it. We seek refuge, healing and affirmation through the material. Social media has connected the world, yet loneliness remains a huge concern. Technology has given us greater freedom and choice, but sometimes we lack the compassion and empathy to treat each other with justice and kindness. We have so much knowledge, yet never have minds been so closed to beliefs that differ.

The material world, and all our modern innovations, simply can't satisfy our insatiable hunger for a higher meaning and purpose. But angels can. Angels offer us sustenance and hope when all else feels lost.

If you define yourself by material things, when those things falter or vanish, what does that say about your sense of self? It suggests that you are wrong and need fixing. It is during those times that it is more important than ever to understand that you are *not* defined by what is material. Your consciousness, your spirit, the loving and mystical part of you that is timeless and perfect, which exists beyond the material, is what defines you, gives you conviction.

Senseless and cruel world events also drive us to seek unseen answers. As far as I know, all the calls from the tragic 9/11 planes spoke only of love. But there is no need to wait for a crisis, personal or collective, to be a catalyst; you can notice and call on your angels right now to find your meaning. And it seems that increasing numbers of people are doing exactly that – recent surveys suggest that at least one in three of us believes in angels.

One of the most exciting developments in recent times has been the ability of angels to adapt themselves. Although the traditional vision of beings with wings and halos remains, this can be limiting, and fewer and fewer people nowadays define them in this way. Angels are no longer confined to religion, saints or statues, or to those who have so-called extraordinary psychic gifts or exclusive knowledge of the angel realms and how to connect to them. Angels are universal and are now flying directly into the lives and hearts of ordinary people.

And once you do find your angels, they won't let you go. They have entered your heart and they won't ever leave.

My love for angels has been the true wonder and joy of my life; and this love calls out to me in really unexpected ways. I pray this book helps you hear and find your angels in your own unexpected ways.

AIM HIGH

Through all my years of research and writing, I know with unshakable certainty that *anyone* can find, hear, see and feel their angels – once they learn how to trust them and turn away from their fears.

Punctuating this book is a selection of the reader stories I've received over the years. I am deeply grateful to the generous people who sent them to me and gave me permission to share their words, experiences and integrity. Names and personal details have been changed in almost all cases to protect their identity.

Although some of the contributors already believed in angels, a fair number did not until their experience. Some are religious, but others are not. Like many people these days, they believe in something higher or greater than themselves existing within and around them but they are not sure if that invisible something is real. And then there are those who believed in nothing at all until an angel came along and changed everything.

They wanted their stories included because they hoped that sharing their experiences would be a source of comfort, guidance and inspiration to others. And I sincerely hope their accounts encourage you to reflect on your own life and recall, perhaps for the first time, life-changing moments you may have previously dismissed but which you may now recognise as the secret work of your angels.

Open your heart and mind to what is revealed. Think of what you are about to discover as your arrow to truth, heaven, bliss, eternity, the afterlife, spirit or whatever name you choose to give to the angelic. This book can point the way and help you to aim high, but it is important you understand that the rest is up to you. You need to be willing to leap.

It is often said the journey of a thousand miles begins with one small step. You've already taken your first step by choosing to be here. In the coming hours, days and months, use what you discover to motivate yourself to continue taking small steady steps in the right direction, until attracting angels becomes a natural part of your life and reflects who you truly are. I'm right here with you in spirit all the way!

Thrilling times lie ahead. Remember, when it comes to finding your angels, stay alert and expect absolutely nothing but the unpredictable. The unseen reality, the invisible force of love that guides and inspires your life has been obscured for far too long. It's high time now to look up and see the truth, the whole truth and nothing but the truth about angels for yourself.

I send you love and an angel to walk beside you.

PART ONE

The Secret World of Angels

'The best and most beautiful things in the world cannot be seen or even touched. They must be felt with the heart.'

HELEN KELLER

CHAPTER ONE

An Angel Called Your Name

In this chapter I share some of my personal history, as well as my angelic experiences. My hope is that you will feel encouraged to ask questions about what you yourself believe to be true about angels.

I was born into poverty. I dropped out of school at sixteen with no qualifications to speak of. Teachers gave up on me and advised me not to bother applying to university. I went into the world of work to make ends meet, but I realised that I still wanted to learn, so I continued my education via home study.

What I'm trying to express is that I certainly wasn't someone destined for a place at the University of Cambridge; but I fell in love with learning, got the required grades and (even though other universities rejected me because my having got my grades through home study was too 'alternative') King's College, Cambridge, made an exception and gave me a chance. I am for ever grateful for that.

My academic credentials from Cambridge certainly helped me get my foot in the door in the publishing world, although it was not easy and for a long time I released my books without any fanfare.

And, although my books were always about spiritual matters, from my teen years onwards I had had many periods of serious doubt that angels were even real.

My family is one of psychics and spiritualists and my relatives could see and hear things from the other side. But not me. I felt like an imposter. My spiritual awakening only really began when my mother died.

About six months after her passing, I had a vivid dream of her, looking ageless and vital. The dreams continued and became more profound, until I had one that I believe saved my life.

In this dream, for the first time since her death, Mum talked to me directly. She told me to take the right path.

Initially, I thought Mum was simply reminding me to follow my heart and be true to myself, as she had always done when she was alive. But the following day I was at a busy traffic junction and I heard her voice, again telling me to take the 'right path'. Without hesitation, I turned the 'wrong' way' for my destination – I turned right rather than left. Moments later, the van in front of me was, tragically, involved in a fatal pile-up.

Angels throughout my life – whether I realised it at the time or not – pulled me back from the brink or gifted me with unexpected inspiration through dreams, hunches, signs and coincidences.

It does often take something major like a bereavement or a personal crisis to kick-start spiritual awakening – the ability to see the remarkable in the ordinary – but you don't need to always be experiencing cutting pain to see your angels.

I had expected my psychic powers to be like a switch that I could just flick on, once I had the right information or learned the correct techniques. I had not understood that spiritual development is really about the growth of the whole person; and this rarely happens overnight. It is a lifelong process of learning to trust your instincts and discovering within yourself courage, determination, patience and humility. It is also about learning to love yourself unconditionally and about letting go of fear – fear of not fitting in, fear of not living up to expectations, fear of death and, above all, fear of what your dreams, hunches and feelings can reveal.

DOUBT SOME MORE

The reason I've shared my experiences of doubt and scepticism is that I wanted you to know that, if you do sometimes feel your angels are far away, this is a well-trodden path. I've been there many times. I may well go there again, but what I have learned is that if I do, it's okay. Doubt can be a catalyst for further spiritual growth. It's not the enemy I thought it was.

When you doubt, you open yourself up to new perspectives and push yourself to discover and learn. Indeed, doubt is the driving force behind every breakthrough. For example, if no one had doubted the world was flat, explorers would not have set out to prove otherwise. It was the people who doubted the voices of authority advising them to stay inside the second tower before a plane struck it on 9/11 that survived. Every episode of doubt in my life so far – as painful as it was – has brought me closer to my angels and reminded me that you don't go to a life in spirit, you *grow* there. And sometimes growth hurts – you are shedding an old skin and being born anew. The fear you feel is just a sign that you need to learn more.

MORE THAN A NAME

Throughout my entire life my angels have been continuously calling my name, protecting me and preparing me. But I realised only recently that a major part of understanding that calling had been hiding in plain sight all along.

My birth name, which I have never shared before as I was estranged from my father, is Paine.

My father's passion was promoting the work of the activist and author of *Common Sense*, Thomas Paine (1737–1809) – my father couldn't prove it, but he believed he was related – and he was secretary of the Thomas Paine Society. Perhaps there is more of my father in me than I have realised before, as my own passion now is to bring a dose of common sense to spirituality.

During the pandemic and the focus on the Black Lives Matter movement, the mission of Thomas Paine kept surfacing, on my newsfeed and in the media. It felt like a sign from the angels; one that I finally allowed myself to recognise.

I know that there are many people who long, as I did, to find their life's meaning, or see their angels, but feel frustrated and disillusioned when nothing seems to come through or they don't feel as though they are making any progress.

If that sounds like you, I'm hoping this book will become a one-stop, how-to guide to understanding that your angels are here and talking to you all the time. You just need to notice them. I want it to be the kind of book you can refer to time and time again, when the going gets tough and doubts, low self-esteem and frustrations creep back in, and you find yourself wondering why you can't see your angels or where all your angels have gone.

THE TOP 10 ANGEL MYTHS

There are some lingering angel myths out there – myths that, if you believe them, can cut you off from discovering their truth and the direct connection to them that is your birthright. Yes, connecting to your angels *is* your birthright. Every one of you reading this has an angel calling your name, wanting you to fulfil your potential. There's evidence to suggest that spirituality, whether we acknowledge or believe in it or not, is in our DNA.[1] So, without further ado, let's clear your way and explode the top 10 angel myths right here, right now.

1. Angels are for the religious

No. This is such an ingrained belief and I need to make it crystal clear that although angels are associated with religion – in particular with Christianity and Islam – they are *not* only for the religious. They are universal. In the early 2000s, British academic Emma Heathcote James conducted a survey[2] of people who believed they had encountered angels. Those who came forward included Christians, Muslims and devotees of other major religions, but around a third said they had no religion and 10 per cent categorised themselves as agnostic or atheist. So if you are religious, angels can slot into your belief system; but you can also love angels if religion is not for you.

2. Angels are beautiful, pale-looking women

No. Even though the qualities associated with angels – love, empathy, kindness – are traditionally regarded as feminine, and many artists depict angels in female form, in films guardian angels typically appear as men, perhaps symbolising the traditional, strong, protective male archetype. Both representations are wrong. Angels don't have any gender. They are spiritual beings, different from humans. When angels appear in human form, they assume either a male or female gender not because they *are* male or female but because they want to shine the spotlight on traditional qualities associated with that gender. And as for being pale-looking, angels transcend race and culture too. I'm mixed race (my mother Indonesian, my father British) and my husband is Chinese but despite this it took the Black Lives Matter movement to alert me fully to the depressing lack of culturally diversity in artistic representations of angels. I hope in coming years this will change.

3. There is no proof

Yes, there is. There is a whole new world of scientific research out there proving that spirit is real, but much of it is hidden in obscure academic and scientific journals. I look forward to introducing you to some of that remarkable research in Chapter Two.

4. Angels have wings and halos

No. Many of us have been conditioned to think of angels in this way as celestial beings are so frequently visually represented like this, but angels can take on an infinite variety of shapes and forms. The definition of an angel experience does not lie in who or what angels are or in how they appear. What defines an angel encounter most is your response to it and whether or not your life is transformed as a result.

And as for those wings, you might be interested to know that, although they feature powerfully in representations, many ancient accounts of angels mention voices, signs and dreams rather than feathers. Up until the fourth century AD, angels in art didn't typically have wings. And halos were not commonly linked to angels until fourth-century Christian representations of them, either. Prior to that halos were associated with pagan gods; it was not until Roman emperors started to have halos painted above their heads as symbols of divinity that angels began to be depicted with halos, too.

And while we are talking about wings and halos, let's also expose all that harp-playing, because this is another inaccurate association. Ancient sources suggest that angels blew trumpets. There is an association between praising divinity and music-making in the Old Testament Psalms, but the angels there play many different instruments. Furthermore, the light that surrounds or emanates from angels in traditional representations is just a symbol of their purity.

To borrow from the iconic film *Fight Club*: the first rule of working with angels is to stop having preconceived ideas about them; and the second rule is to stop having preconceived ideas about what you think they should look, sound and feel like! Angels appear in infinite ways and no individual angel looks the same as another. If you have a strong affinity with the traditional representation of angels – with wings and halos – they may appear to you in that way, but you see angels in whatever way you need to see them at that time.

5. You have to be a good or 'pure' person to see angels

No. Angels don't just speak to saints, monks or extremely kind people. You don't have to be perfect to see angels, just human. And every human, even saints (Mother Teresa often spoke of her struggles to be good, or what she called her 'dark night of the soul') are a complex mixture of good and not so good.

So, if you feel a bit of a fake and that you are not worthy of angelic attention because you know how often you let your halo slip, you are no different from anyone else. You are simply being human, and any human can be kind. There is no entry qualification for connecting to your angels. Just start doing it and see how it makes you feel.

6. It's too late

No, it's not. Perhaps you feel you are set in your ways and it's too late for you to see angels or to behave like one. Let's explode this myth with a true-life example. In 2020, UK war veteran Captain Tom Moore was about to celebrate his 100th birthday. He decided to do a fund-raising event to celebrate and raise money for health workers at the same time. He set himself a modest target of £1,000 and promised family and friends online that he would walk laps around his garden with his walking frame until he achieved it. But little did he know that thousands of people around the world would find out about his efforts. To date he has raised more than £32 million (US$41 million). He also received over 125,000 birthday cards on his birthday and has been awarded a knighthood. You are never too old to do the work of angels.

7. Only gullible people believe in angels

Well, there is a tendency for sensitive souls to be trusting, to believe what they are told without question. But the true stories in this book show clearly that these sensitive souls have intelligence and courage, too. Courage because, as each story makes clear, believing in angels, acting with love, compassion and integrity, saying and doing the right thing, speaking out when there is injustice takes true grit, real inner strength. Sensitive is the new strong! And angels aren't for those with low self-esteem either. Without self-love and the ability to think your own thoughts, angels struggle to find a lasting home in your heart and your life.

8. You need to believe in angels to see them

No. Belief helps but it is not essential. You may be surprised to learn that you don't need to believe in angels to feel their magic. I've had many messages from people who did not believe in angels, but then something extraordinary happened to change their mind.

9. Only people with extraordinary ability can see angels

No. No. No.

Yes, there are people who describe themselves as psychics, clairvoyants, mediums, angel healers and lightworkers. The connotation with these terms is of 'special' psychic powers unavailable to the majority of us. However, the reason for the clear vision of these people is not that they are special – it is simply that they have decided to focus their energy on their psychic development.

Thinking you need to be a psychic or a medium to see angels is the same as asking if you need to be human to see angels. All of us have the same mystic potential.[3]

10. It's complicated.

Again, not in my opinion, and in Chapter Two I explode this rather toxic assumption.

Connecting to angels is the *simplest* and most natural thing to do. Yet, as is often the case, something that should be simple has become overcomplicated. In my opinion, dependency on any spiritual system, teacher or guru becomes a barrier and makes it harder for your angels to reach you. Sure, there are techniques you can learn, such as meditation, visualisation and ritual work, but as this book reveals, these techniques are delightfully straightforward, and you can easily learn them yourself.

SO, ARE YOU TRULY READY TO FLY?

The next two chapters further reveal the mystery and science of angels and bring you fully up to date with celestial beings as they are appearing today. They also prove to you once and for all that *anyone,* regardless of whether or not they have what are often called psychic or mediumistic gifts, can see angels.

In essence, every word you will read from this point onwards will remind you that there is absolutely nothing stopping you from seeing your own your angels *now*.

And if you still don't feel ready, if you still doubt yourself, trust me – I've been there myself so many times – it's just another sign that you truly are ready.

CHAPTER TWO

The Science of Angels

Who do you think angels are?

Whenever you hear the word 'angel', chances are it makes you feel lighter in some unexplained way. But what exactly does that word mean?

MUST BE AN ANGEL

In essence, angels are messengers.

In ancient Hebrew, Arabic and Greek the word 'angel' translated always means 'messenger', whether that word is used with religious associations – as a messenger of the unseen or divine – or outside a specific religion, as an embodiment of goodness and unconditional love.

They are typically perceived as spiritual beings of pure light, resembling humans in form but with flashing eyes, floating hair, a beautiful face and a giant pair of wings with a halo to match. They belong to an invisible dimension and therefore defy science, logic and reason. And entwined with this familiar presentation exists the belief that angels are also a force of goodness and love in the world, a spiritual light that exists within us all.

Although there is disagreement about their substance and form, in every culture, religion and tradition there is widespread agreement about their role as messengers from the world of spirit – the unseen realm also known as the afterlife, heaven, or whatever term you choose to describe sensations, feelings, memories and dreams that exist beyond the material world or your five senses. Typically (but not always), these messages are invisible. But even though they can't always be clearly seen, 'proven' or understood, they still feel intensely real to those who experience them.

As messengers, angels embody, manifest, express or reveal a deeper purpose.

Seen in this light, surely anything that brings a message of deeper meaning, whether a vision, dream, an intuition, a coincidence, the timely appearance of a white feather or anything else that reminds you there is more to this life than the material, can be described as angelic? This expansive but personal interpretation is how I have come to define angels.

But I can't stress enough here that it doesn't matter so much what *I* believe but what *you* believe. I strongly urge you to think more about your own definition of angels. Get curious! Indeed, your willingness to open your mind to consider what angels mean to you is your first real step to connecting authentically to them. It is often said that love and compassion define a spiritual person, but curiosity is the real foundation stone – curiosity to learn more and to constantly add to your knowledge of angels.

I truly believe that angels keep themselves elusive and are so hard to define because they want you to discover what they are for *yourself*. Angels shape-shift to speak in ways understandable to you and *only* you.

Across the world and through time, they are variously named as *devas, diamones, valkyries, kuribu, fereshta* . . . and many other things, but they are really all one and the same: spiritual forces that connect humans to the love and light inside and around them.

Mystical birds that travel from this life to the next in search of a person's soul feature in shamanic cultures, such as those of the First Nations in North America.

The equivalent of angels in Buddhism, which is often regarded as a philosophy rather than a faith, are the *bodhisattvas*, who reveal themselves as forms of light or through meditation and whose mission is to help others find enlightenment.

There are numerous records of angels as a strong spiritual force independent of established religion. Great mystics, such as St Thomas Aquinas (1226–74) and the poet Dante (1265–1321), spoke of angel visions. And when the scientific revolution seriously challenged religion, angels as creative inspirations were fiercely championed by the Swedish mystic Emanuel Swedenborg (1688–1772) and the English Romantic poets, chiefly William Blake (1757–1827).

Since the 1960s the spiritual but non-religious New Age movement has been steadily gathering momentum and is enthusiastically embraced by the millennial generation, leading many to term New Age, an on-trend Now Age. This movement seeks inspiration from a mix of ancient pagan, Celtic and gnostic spirituality and Eastern mysticism, united by the theme of personal transformation. Unlike religions, it has no prophets, sacred texts or creeds.

Not surprisingly, given its free-flowing form, the New Age movement has welcomed angels, who have flown right into its heart and are regarded by many as its leading lights.

In my opinion then, beings of light appearing as they do throughout history, in all religions and in contexts outside religion, illustrates the willingness of angels to adapt themselves to speak without prejudice to any heart willing to welcome them.

SPIRITUAL SCIENCE

Belief in angels has always been with us and today scientists are taking that belief seriously and researching angelic encounters and experiences. Science has moved forward in leaps and bounds in recent years, especially in the fields of consciousness research, precognition, mediumship, channelling, energy-healing and near-death experiences.

Unfortunately, as mentioned earlier, much of the research hasn't made it into the mainstream and instead lies hidden in science journals; and the use of complicated scientific jargon makes it inaccessible. It is a very positive step, though, that modern science is finally overcoming its aversion to exploring what is irrational, mysterious and unseen. Here's what scientists now are discovering about angelic experiences.

NEAR-DEATH EXPERIENCES (NDES)

A 2014 study on 2,000 patients from hospitals all over the world was led by leading resuscitation expert Dr Sam Parnia. Parnia does not believe in life after death but, being a resuscitation expert, he was prompted to study NDEs scientifically because of the many experiences his patients reported to him after they had been on the brink of death.[4]

The study has proved that consciousness – what we might also call soul or spirit – can survive for up to three minutes after bodily death. The research was so conclusive that another ongoing study is being funded.

MEDIUMSHIP

In 2015 the Windbridge Research Center team published a study[5] involving fifty-eight readings with twenty mediums who volunteered to be tested under strict scientific conditions, eliminating all possibility of 'cold reading' or fraud. This study is regarded as strong evidence for the reception of anomalous information by mediums – in other words, mediums reporting accurate information about dead people without any previous knowledge of those people or the sitters.

CONSCIOUSNESS RESEARCH

Leading the world in consciousness research is the Institute of Noetic Sciences (IONS), with a team of highly qualified scientists that includes Dr Arnaud Delorme,[6] who pioneered EEG technology; Dr Dean Radin;[7] Dr Loren Carpenter[8] (who as well as being a physicist just happens to be a double Oscar winner, co-founder of Pixar Studios and Science Director at Disney);

Dr Garret Yount;[9] and IONS research director, Dr Helané Wahbeh.[10] Together they are conducting studies[11] showing that paranormal experiences at the very least deserve scientific investigation, as people have been having them since the beginning of time and continue to do so. They are part of the human experience and need to be treated as data; and what the team at IONS is finding is that when such experiences are studied scientifically, in a large majority of cases there is every reason to believe the explanation could be paranormal.

CHANNELLING

This is the ability to access information and energy not limited by space and time. It is a phenomenon that has been recorded throughout history and in different cultures. There is experimental evidence that some information that is channelled could not come from any known source. For example, Edgar Cayce[12] was a trance channel, the term used for someone who allows a spiritual being to speak through them directly, and a number of his predictions have been verified; and for many years the US government funded StarGate,[13] a parapsychology research unit investigating psychic abilities. For the past few years, the IONS channelling research programme[14] pioneered by IONS director of research Helané Wahbeh has been demonstrating that some channels can receive verifiable information they could not have access to otherwise. Through researching channelling the IONS scientists hope to learn more about how consciousness can transcend the human body.

PRESENTIMENT

This is the scientific term for an intuitive feeling about the future. Studies[15] that measure bodily reactions to future events have had encouraging results, suggesting that intuition (extrasensory perception, ESP, or 'spidey sense' as it is called by the US military, who have funded serious research[16] into sixth sense) is a superpower. Precognition or remote viewing studies[17] that test perception beyond the limitations of space and time have revealed surprisingly positive outcomes and support from unlikely sources. A psychologist from Cornell University, Daryl Bem, popularised this research.[18] And Dr Jessica Utts, Professor of Statistics at the University of California and President of the American Statistical Association, is on record[19] as saying in her presidential address, attended by thousands of statisticians from all over the world, that precognition appears to work. She referenced research done on a classified project for the US government (from 1978 to 1995) to see if precognition and other related phenomena might be used for intelligence gathering during the Cold War. She stated that the supportive data was quite strong statistically and, if it pertained to something more mundane, would be widely accepted. She pleaded for scientists to stop rejecting the data and research in this area because, contrary to popular belief, psychic abilities do not contradict what is already known by science.

TELEPATHY

Research[20] on pairs of people isolated from one another, using an experimental protocol called *ganzfield* (a technique used in parapsychology to detect potential psychic ability) to test the existence of conscious telepathy (mind reading), has been repeated many times by researchers (some of whom were highly sceptical), many times yielding successful effects. Popularising this research is famous scientist and author, Rupert Sheldrake, with his research[21] on the telepathic bonds between humans and animals.

MIND–BODY

Scientific discoveries about the biochemical effects of the brain's functioning suggest that the cells of your body are affected by your thoughts. This new science of epigenetics is revolutionising our understanding of the interconnected link between mind and body and is being popularised by the likes of renowned cell biologist, Dr Bruce Lipton.[22]

MIND OVER MATTER

Random number generators (RNGs) are laboratory instruments used to test whether mental intention can affect random outcomes. Previously this was done with dice, but RNGs ensure true random events and the results are encouraging. Global consciousness research is a worldwide version of an RNG experiment that tests to see the effects of focused attention by large numbers of people at the same time.[23] Results over the last twenty years show odds against chance greater than a trillion to one.[24]

ENERGY HEALING

A study completed in 2020 by the Institute of Noetic Sciences (IONS)[25] looked at energy medicine and its effect on pain. The study found significant positive results in pain relief and other outcomes. Other studies on the power of intention[26] suggest that blessings and prayers may have slightly beneficial effects.

AFTERLIFE ENCOUNTERS

It was a revelation to me when I discovered that scientists are starting to investigate seriously visions and signs believed to be from the other side. In 2016 the American Psychological Association published a groundbreaking book called *Transcendent Mind*,[27] which offers a powerful argument that the mind (consciousness) might be able to exist separately from the brain and body. If that is possible, then it offers a theory for the possibility of life after death, afterlife experiences, near-death experiences, out-of-body experiences and past and future life recall. (A pioneer in the scientific evaluation of reincarnation, who collated compelling stories of past life recall, was University of Virginia professor Dr Ian Stephenson.[28])

And alongside the ongoing research at parapsychology departments in universities and organisations dedicated to psychic research all over the world, there are also independent organisations breaking new ground, such as the Galileo Report project[29] and psychologist Dr Gary Schwartz's SoulPhone Foundation technology.[30] And I should also give an appreciative nod to the underground community of paranormal investigators (ghost hunters), who are scientifically investigating reports of paranormal activity.

DREAMS

There's promising research for the healing and even predictive power of dreams. See Chapter Seven.

* * *

Incredulous that such mind-opening research and data wasn't more widely available, I reached out to the various scientists and institutions leading these studies. I was delighted when some agreed to talk to me. Although there are respected parapsychology research departments in leading universities all over the world, as well as many esteemed international organisations pioneering consciousness and 'psychic world' or 'psi' research (see Resources, page 213), the organisation that felt most accessible to a non-scientist like me was the Institute of Noetic Sciences or IONS. Indeed, my interviews with the entire IONS science team eventually formed the basis for Season 1 of my podcast, *White Shores*.

OUT THERE, IN HERE

IONS was founded in 1973 by American astronaut Dr Edgar Mitchell. Nearly fifty years ago, Mitchell became the sixth person to walk on the moon. As his mission came to an end, however, he discovered an entirely new purpose – one that would define his life for decades to come. Travelling back from the moon and with the Earth in sight, he was enveloped by a profound sense of universal connectedness. In his own words:

> *I realized that the story of ourselves as told by science – our cosmology, our religion – was incomplete and likely flawed. I recognized that the Newtonian idea of separate, independent, discrete things in the universe wasn't a fully accurate description. What was needed was a new story of who we are and what we are capable of becoming.*

Mitchell's transformative experience led him to establish IONS. He understood that by applying the scientific rigour used in his explorations of outer space, we could better understand the mysteries of inner space – the space in which he felt an undeniable sense of interconnection and oneness. Mitchell passed away in 2016 but IONS[31] continues his work. The science team there use the power of science to explore our inner space, understanding that both objective knowledge and subjective knowing are necessary for a more complete understanding.

Here's a mind-opening thought: Mitchell walked on the moon, but what felt more astonishing to him was his inner journey, his transcendent experience. There's such a powerful lesson here that what we seek isn't 'out there', it's right here within us.

'Noetic' is a scientific term used to describe the unseen power of the mind, the inner world, and tuning into information and energy not limited by space and time. The way in which that information is accessed can be called our 'noetic signature'. It's a different approach obviously as the researchers at IONS are scientists – but it's crystal clear to me that discovering our noetic signature is what I have been referring to all these years in my spiritual writing as 'angel talk'.

You may wonder if all these scientists researching consciousness in this bold way are believers and approach everything with personal bias. But that could not be further than the truth. Dr Parnia, the leading NDE researcher, does not believe in the afterlife. And, whenever I have interviewed scientists in this field about their personal beliefs, the majority have been reluctant to commit. They told me they were scientists first and believers or sceptics second. The integrity of the research mattered more to them than proving a point.

I want as many people as possible to know that the world of science is beginning to consider the very real possibility that there is an unseen element to our lives – that our dreams and hunches are real.

I also want you to know that belief in the afterlife and the paranormal is far more widespread than you might think; polls[32] typically show that up to 70 per cent of people do believe in life after death. And people from all walks of life, some perhaps surprising, have beliefs or are open to the idea of the afterlife and the paranormal; this is something I've looked into myself.[33] Not to mention that some brilliant, Nobel-prize-winning scientists past and present, such as Professor Brian Josephson, Alan Turing, Max Planck and Wolfgang Pauli to name but a few, have been open-minded about the paranormal.

MOST COMMON ANGEL QUESTIONS

I want to end this chapter with a few questions I'm often asked about angels.

What do you say to sceptics?

I welcome debates with sceptics – as some examples, listen to my appearance on Russell Brand's podcast *Under the Skin*, where he questions me very intensely. I also welcomed it with open arms when *Guardian* journalist and sceptic Michael Marshall invited me onto his *Be Reasonable* podcast[34] and also when I sparred with the highly sceptical Piers Morgan on *GMTV*.

I know all the rational and psychological explanations against the reality of angels, and I don't try to convince sceptics or anyone else to believe in them. What I do is to share with them what science is revealing about the nature of angelic experiences. I also point to the database of angel stories that I have gathered over the years. Anecdotal, yes; but in a court of law witness statements are presented as evidence.

I would ask a sceptic, too, to think about the power of love, empathy and kindness. These are invisible forces that are real even though they can't be seen or measured scientifically. What proves their existence is the transformative impact they have on a person's life. It is the same with angels.

And even the most sceptical person will concede that there is much in this life we cannot explain. Why are we here? What is life? To date scientists can't answer these and other questions.

Consider, too, what we are taught in school about space being infinite. How do scientists know that for sure? They don't. And what is infinity? Something that never ends? Sounds pretty magical and unscientific to me. It also raises the question that if space can be infinite, why can't our spirits?

So, whenever I debate with sceptics, I have as many questions to ask them and just as much desire for answers and proof from them as they have from me!

Why is quantum theory increasingly being linked with spirituality?

There is currently much talk in New Age/spiritual circles about quantum science, but quantum theory in itself does not suggest that angels exist. However, there have been drawn, by pioneering scientists, some fascinating links between modern physics and mysticism. One idea, first posited in the early twentieth century by physicist Max Planck, is that the universe consists of more than physical matter; and it also includes packets of energy that are not continuous but unpredictable. So while from a rational, logical perspective, angels are not real, from a quantum perspective they are simply things we don't yet understand well enough.

There is a lot of discussion and activity about angels on social media. Do the two go together?

Social media can be an immediate and positive way to recognise and remind yourself of your angels. The sight of an angel image in your newsfeed can be a helpful prompt to remind you always to choose what is right and true. And we all know it is quite easy to get carried away or express yourself a bit too forcefully online; so before you click (or say or do) anything, ask yourself if your guardian angel would approve. In these ways you can use social media for good, to help you to keep connecting with your angels.

Should I be talking to anyone but God?

Many people who believe in angels, myself included, are spiritual and not religious. But if your faith forbids you talking to anyone but God, your angels won't be offended. Remember, angels adapt to whatever is in your best interests. They are loving expressions of all that is pure, so it could be said that when you are talking to God, you are also talking to your angels. If you believe you have angels watching over you, this is not to deny God but to have faith in the awesome power of goodness and love, however that force is embodied for you.

How do angels appear?

Angels are non-denominational, non-gender and non-racial, and they can appear in any form or way that makes sense to the observer. How they appear depends on personal history – your culture, your beliefs, your religion if you have one – and your level of spiritual awareness. This is why someone who is religious may see them with wings and a halo, whereas someone who is not may view them as shapes in the clouds.

Most of us see them in our dreams, hear them in our thoughts or sense them through our feelings. Or they come to us through gentle signs such as the unexpected appearance of a white feather. They can also appear through the conscious or unconscious guidance and the kindness of others. And sometimes they can manifest through the spirits of departed loved ones. That's why in my books, the term angel is often interchangeable with the term spirit.

What do you feel about giving angels names, or different types of angels?

I'm ambivalent. In my books I know I encourage you to talk and connect to angels of growth, angels of change, angels of relationships, angels of healing, angels of communication, angels of letting go, angels of tears, angels of joy, angels of trust, angels of dreams, angels of hope, angels of nature, angels of detachment, angels of patience, angels of memory, angels of truth, angels of tolerance, angels of love . . . But I don't think of them as different angels. I regard them as all one and the same, all interconnected.

There are many different terms used for angels. But in a nutshell, the term 'angel' refers broadly to the loving presence or force – sometimes visible but more likely to be invisible – that acts as a connection to spirit. Put another way, angels exist within us, around us. A guardian angel is believed to be with each of us from before conception. They accompany us through everything we think, say and do in this life, and remain with us when we pass into the next. They watch and advise. They can be thought of as our 'conscience' or 'intuition'.

The term 'spirit' refers to the spirits of people, which live on after their death. This is not the same thing as angels – angels have never had a physical life here on Earth – but angels do sometimes choose to express themselves through the spirits of departed loved ones.

As for naming angels, the angels understand that we humans sometimes need to give them names or characteristics to help our understanding of them. You can ask your inner angel to reveal their name, or give them a name that inspires you – perhaps simply look online for an infinite variety of angel names for every need and season.

Anything that helps you become more aware of your angels and more open to their guidance is a step in the right direction. So, if you want to give your guardian angel a name, rest assured you have their blessing. My advice, though, is to avoid the bewildering choice of angel and archangel names out there and simply go for a name you love, and that feels right to you (see appendix for more clarity on angel terms). I love this story about angel names from Shelley.[35]

My first angelic encounter was fifteen years ago now, and life is truly beautiful as I have been blessed by angels since that very day. Angels still surprise me now. It turns out that

I am not destined to have a 'celebrity' angel by my side – at first, when I was creating my angelic connections, I thought I was hearing the name 'Michael', but in reality, I was hearing 'Muriel'. My purple angel, Muriel. We do not always get what we expect in life, but we always receive what we need when we open our heart and mind to the best possible outcome.

As for angels associated with certain days, times, seasons or signs and so on, there is no right name, so just go with what resonates with you. There are thousands and thousands of angel names, all of them beautiful, from every religion, culture and lore. Your inner angel knows which angel is calling your name because the specific qualities associated with them may be ones you need to develop or ones that can help you heal or offer comfort.

And if none of the names you encounter speaks to you, why not be original, as angels long for you to be, and make up your own magical name?

Can human beings be angels?

We often use the word 'angel' to describe someone who is compassionate and kind. I believe that we can all do the work of angels and that they can work their magic through people, including you, so in this respect yes, humans can be earth angels. Every day, health care workers and other good Samaritans are bringing angels closer to earth.

Why don't angels stop bad things happening to good people? Perhaps the answer will always remain incomprehensible to the human mind. Perhaps there is a bigger picture and when there is injustice and cruelty it is part of a person's soul plan or destiny. Who knows?

Sometimes we learn the most through struggle. Our angels may shed a tear with us, but they know they must not intervene so that our souls evolve. So if you are struggling, as long as you are learning, you are growing and the meaning of your life is to grow and learn. You may not realise it but you are still living your meaning during times of struggle. What your angels can do if you choose to notice or reach out to them is send you the spiritual strength to cope and the understanding that life is constantly changing, emotions are not static and, however negative you may feel right now, 'this too shall pass.'

Life probably shouldn't be easy, because we don't tend to learn and grow if we remain in our comfort zone. We learn and grow – reveal who we truly are from the inside out – when times are challenging. Indeed, perhaps we should never stop asking why. Perhaps the power is not in the answer but in the asking. Think about it. We know why a woman screams in pain during childbirth so we are not overly concerned. If we knew the reason for bad things happening it's entirely possible we would become as nonchalant. We would no longer flex our empathy and compassion muscles. Is that a world you would want to live in?

Do even those who've done wrong have guardian angels, and are they punished for their wrongdoing?

This is a complicated area but, put simply, while it is not accurate to talk about punishment when it comes to angels, the angels do wish to teach us all empathy. Studies and stories of near-death experiences suggest that in spirit, the learning never stops. You take your spirit with you to the other side and will feel everything you have made others feel on Earth.

So a wrongdoer will not find peace on the other side until they have truly felt and so understood the impact of their actions.

In essence, in every moment of your life you are creating the kind of afterlife you will experience.

Does my guardian angel see everything I do?

Yes. You may find this rather an alarming thought! We all have done things we are not proud of in our lives; but your guardian angel loves you unconditionally and knows that spiritual growth often involves encounters with darkness. If you didn't look into this darkness from time to time, how would you know how to recognise the light? Life is all about making the right choices and your guardian angel knows that wisdom only comes from learning from your choices, even if they are bad ones that cause regret and pain.

Ask yourself each time you say or do something, is it something that you would want to watch again on the other side in a life review? Is it something your guardian angel would approve of?

Why can't I see my angels?

The point is not why can't you see them, but how can you nonetheless communicate with and receive wisdom and love from them?

And the answer is: simply keep your mind, heart and eyes open to the wonder all around and within you. Be receptive, curious, patient and kind. They will come when you are ready.

PERFECT PREPARATION

Before we move on to practical ways you can see, hear and sense angels, the next chapter will help you achieve the receptive state of mind most conducive to angel work. It will reveal true stories from people who, like you, are finding their own way to their truth. Relax and enjoy the comfort their stories bring – and let them act as perfect preparation for welcoming angels into your own life.

CHAPTER THREE

Talking Angels

Angels inspire us to be stronger and greater than we think we can be and, for those who believe, just thinking about their comforting presence is life-transforming. As representatives of what is good and loving in virtually every religion, tradition and culture, they have – unsurprisingly – inspired some of the world's greatest mystics and artists.

Before I remind you of a few famous angel encounters and introduce a collection of true stories that showcase the way angels are appearing to people today, pause a while and reflect on representations of angels in art, film and culture more widely. Maybe think of angels in imagery, films, songs, and anything else that speaks to you. Cultivating this receptive mindset prepares you perfectly for the angel-attracting techniques introduced in Part Two.

It's outside the scope of this book to delve very deeply into the impact of angels on culture. The purpose of this section is to fill your mind and heart with angel inspirations and to encourage you to notice them everywhere. The more attention you pay to angels, the more likely you are to see their footprints.

ANGEL ART

Perhaps there is a specific angel image that makes your heart sing? If not, why not find one? Or if you can't find anything suitable, draw or create an angel image for yourself.

There is a whole world of angel art out there, in every tradition and culture, for you to discover and be inspired by. If you get a chance to visit a gallery, on or offline, that houses any great angel artwork, seize it. Great art inspires a sense of awe that can help you establish clearer channels between you and your angels.

Memorable angel images can also be found in many a graveyard and church. And angel representations can also be found in non-religious contexts. For example, in the United Kingdom, the *Angel of the North* is a massive contemporary steel structure (wider than the height of the Statue of Liberty) well worth seeing. Even though it has no facial features nor a halo, it is instantly recognisable as an angel.

One of the most inspirational musical works of all time – Handel's *Messiah*, composed in 1741 – was inspired by a vision of angels. You may already have your favourite angel anthem but if not, why not open yourself to finding one now? Look for a song that speaks to your heart. Abba's 'I Believe in Angels' and 'Angels', written by Robbie Williams and Ray Heffernan, are hugely and endlessly popular.

Angels have also inspired great poets and writers throughout history. British poet, painter and printmaker William Blake (1757–1827) believed much of the inspiration for his art came from his lifelong encounters with angels. And the words of Mary

Frye's immortal 'Do Not Stand at My Grave and Weep': *'I am not there, I do not sleep. I am a thousand winds that blow,'* . . . *'I am the soft stars that shine at night'* . . . *'I am not there. I did not die,'* encapsulate the eternal essence of angels.

And how about 'Air and Angels' (1633) by John Donne?

Angels have also inspired great literature; for example, the works of J. R. R. Tolkien (1892–1973), who in turn influenced J. K. Rowling when writing her Harry Potter books.

One of the most inspiring and unforgettable angel films has to be *It's a Wonderful Life* (1946). And angels play their part in many other films and TV shows. Look out for them. They may not be so obviously there as is Clarence in *It's a Wonderful Life*, but remember they are shape-shifters. Aren't many of our much-loved 'superheroes' simply archetypes of our guardian angels? They are beings with superhuman powers, whose identity is uncertain, but who resemble humans and who work selflessly for the forces of justice and goodness.

The blissful Disney film *Up* is a study in coping with bereavement. And the *Frozen* films symbolise the journey to self-love and the importance of doing the next right thing. These are both qualities that angels can encourage in you. Also, the wonderful Disney Pixar film *Soul* showcases all the afterlife and angel themes covered in *The Truth About Angels*, in particular that meaning isn't found where you think it is.

And in the world of TV, I find Ricky Gervais's *Afterlife* deeply spiritual. You can find angels in what might seem like the most unexpected places.

FAMOUS ANGEL ENCOUNTERS

St Joan of Arc (1412–31) had angelic visions and heard mystic voices from the age of thirteen and overcame social and gender barriers. She seems from our perspective to be light years ahead of her time. And St Francis of Assisi (1181–1226) saw angels and set an example of courage, kindness and peace.

The message of 'angels within and around us', as Emmanuel Swedenborg (1688–1772) recorded in his books (which he believed he channelled with the help of angels), influenced many writers and artists, including Blake, Goethe and Dostoyevsky. Swedenborg taught that, although we don't realise it, angels exist within us already while we are living on Earth.

Not enough people know that the first US President, George Washington (1732–99) had a vision of his country's future in which an angel spoke to him and revealed the destiny of the United States.

And aviator Charles Lindbergh (1902–74) revealed, years after his incredible solo, non-stop flight across the Atlantic Ocean in May 1927, that on his flight he had been accompanied by a host of angels who had talked to him, reassured him and brought him home safely. In his memoir he acknowledged that his vision could be dismissed by reason and logic, but the 'longer I live, the more limited I believe rationality to be.'

Wounded soldiers from the Battle of the Somme in August 1914, during World War One, told nurses that they had seen angels on the battlefield. What is interesting about these 'angels of Mons', as they are known, and illustrative of angels' ability to shape-shift and assume forms that speak to each observer personally, is that French soldiers said they saw Archangel Michael riding a white horse, while the British saw St George in golden armour on a white horse.

So, angels can impact and transcend history and inspire people to believe in their own potential for healing, forgiveness – and even greatness. Often the primary motivation of great artists, musicians, writers, statesmen, engineers, philosophers, poets, teachers and heroes is to help, guide, lead, amaze or inspire others. This loving intention is so strong that it allows the angel within them to break free from limitations, fly high and overcome seemingly insurmountable obstacles, traumas and problems.

Seen in this light all of us are capable of genius, of rising above the ordinary and the most difficult or traumatic obstacles that life throws in our path – if we simply allow ourselves to express, without interference, the loving intentions (or put otherwise, the angels) that we already have inside ourselves.

ANGELS TODAY

Time now to get and stay present.

Advances in resuscitation techniques in the last few decades mean that more people are being brought back from the brink of death and are able to share their experiences.

Heaven Is for Real (2010), later transformed into a film, is the compelling, true story of a young child's near-death experience.

That story was rooted in Christian belief, but

Harvard-educated neurosurgeon, Dr Eben Alexander, with his provocatively titled memoir *Proof of Heaven* (2012), showcased his non- religious spiritual universal message of angels.

As well as true stories of near-death experiences, more and more books that present the science precisely and with an open mind are becoming mainstream bestsellers. There is *Surviving Death* (2017) by *New York Times* bestselling author and investigative journalist Leslie Kean (now a hugely popular 2021 Netflix documentary), who, after setting out the facts, comes to the conclusion that it is extremely likely *something* interesting happens when we die. Dr Dean Radin's bestseller *Real Magic* is another tour de force guide that presents the science of the paranormal in an accessible and credible way.

As well as the stories that are turned into books and films, there are wonderful and compelling stories of the experiences of the people you are about to encounter later in this chapter.

For me the truth about angels is found in peoples' stories illustrating the ordinary but extraordinary ways angels have spoken to them.

As my readers know, I have collated these everyday angel stories over the years and shared them with as wide an audience as possible. Every story I am sent is a gift, a unique and remarkable miracle, but here is a typical selection – if anything about angels can ever be described as 'typical' – to illustrate some of the gentle ways that angels are reaching out.

David's story: *I was drifting off to sleep when, in my mind's eye, an image of my departed best friend shone through brightly. He died two years ago. We were close. He was best man at my wedding. With my eyes closed I saw him as clear as day. He was saying things to me and looked very animated. I couldn't hear or understand anything he said but he was so alive. I opened my eyes expecting to see him but there was no one there. I closed my eyes and there he was again, so vital and alive. I kept my eyes tightly closed for as long as possible as I didn't want to lose sight of him again. I 'saw' him for several minutes and then he faded away waving.*

The experience was surreal but it also felt real. I can only describe it as similar to watching a movie but with the movie projected onto the backs of your eyelids. It was not alarming or unnatural. It felt normal. I have often thought about my best friend and wished I could have seen him one more time to say goodbye. I got my wish. It has really helped me cope with the loss of my best friend.

Whether a vision is seen with our eyes closed, as in the story above from David and the other stories below, or with our eyes open, the impact on the observer seems the same. They emerge from the experience with the certain knowledge that their loved one is alive and at peace and that perhaps, just perhaps, life goes on after the body dies.

Samantha's story: *After reading about dreams and, on your recommendation, placing a pen and notepad beside my bed to record them immediately on waking, I woke up one morning and wrote down all I could remember from my dreams. About an hour later I got in touch with a friend, who told me that a mutual and wonderful acquaintance of ours had died during the night. This acquaintance had walked through my dreams that night. I had called out to her and she had replied, 'Hi Sa,' which is what she habitually called me. She had been wearing familiar clothes. When my friend told me that our lovely acquaintance had passed away, I felt so sad, but grateful that I got to see her smile and wave to me one last time in my dream.*

Mira's story: *I feel like my husband's transition to spirit has already happened. He is alive in body, but his dementia has taken him from me now. He doesn't recognise me. Watching someone you love fade away before your eyes is beyond traumatic. I have cried myself to sleep night after night, but my angels found a way to give me the strength to care for him, myself and my family.*

Last year when my husband still had moments of lucidity, I had a dream a week before his birthday, and in my dream my husband was in space. He was in the stars. He told me he was happy there and I should make him glow. Those were his exact words. When I woke, I knew what I had to do.

I went online and purchased a star for my husband. I called the star Luke because that's his middle name and he always said he preferred Luke to his real name, Ben. I looked up the meaning of the name and it means, 'A bright glowing light.' When I gifted my husband the star for his birthday, his eyes lit up. He asked me to call him Luke from now on. It was one of the last special moments of vivid recognition between us.

Today my husband is still alive in body, but he doesn't recognise me or our children. There are no more moments of lucidity. I love and care for him as best I can and whenever I need to vent, I seek out his star in the night sky and talk to it with my heart and soul. I've discovered a new interest in astronomy and his supernova star is in the constellation of Hercules. Knowing he is forever up there is such a comfort and source of strength to me. I know he is up there. He's my angel watching over me.

Jeremy's story: *Last year, I lost my first-born son. His death was unexpected. He had an undiagnosed malignant brain tumour. Within days the light of my life was gone. He was just fourteen years old. The pain for myself and my wife has been unbearable. The toughest time is during the night. The routine of daily life and the demands of our younger son (he's only four) keeps us grounded during the day. But during the night the tears fall.*

One night, about six months after his passing, my wife had finally managed to fall asleep but I couldn't. I got up to make myself a hot drink. I went and sat in the living room and found myself scrolling my phone looking through the photo album at pictures of my son. My face was wet with tears within moments. I noticed that the lights in the hall were switched on. I was sure I hadn't switched them on when I got up as I didn't want them to wake my wife. So I got up and switched them off, before returning to the kitchen.

No sooner had I sat down than the lights switched on again. This had never happened before. My wife was asleep and my younger son couldn't reach the switch. I got up to switch them off again but this time memories came flooding back of all the times I had tiptoed into the hall to switch the lights off before. You see my departed son was scared of the dark and until he was about eleven, he had insisted we keep the hall light on at night until he fell asleep because it comforted him. We happily obliged and when we went to bed ourselves and knew he was fast asleep we would switch the lights off.

The lights have never switched on by themselves like that before and they haven't since. My wife has also told me that sometimes she feels our departed son kiss her cheek before she goes to sleep. I am convinced these are clear signs from my son. He's an angel now and comforting me, just as I used to comfort him when he was afraid of the dark.

Ruby's story: *Charlotte was only four years old when she died. I think about her every second of every day. I miss her every time my heart beats, but the grief and torment I felt has been replaced by a sense of comfort. Let me explain.*

Charlotte was fantastic at drawing for one so young. She was forever scribbling and handing me pictures of stick men and women. In the months before she died, she'd include rainbows in almost all of her pictures. She even drew snow people with rainbows hovering over them. When I asked her why, she just laughed and said that you can have rainbows anywhere you want to.

I don't want to go into the details of her unexpected death as some things hurt so much, but I do want to tell you about her funeral. I woke up on the day of her funeral numb with shock and aching with grief. My mum had to help me get dressed, as I was shaking so much and could barely stand. I wanted my little girl back. I would have given my life to have my little girl back. I regretted all those times I had sent her back to bed when she couldn't sleep. Why hadn't I held her, savoured every precious second? I longed for some kind of sign from her that she was okay and that she was in a place where there was only love and joy. I prayed for a sign but resigned myself to the fact that I wasn't going to get one. Real life didn't work that way.

It was raining hard as we drove towards the church, yet I barely noticed. Everything seemed bleak and grey now; the world had lost its colour without her in it and even if the sun had been out it would still have felt like rain to me. We stood there with our umbrellas, as her little coffin was lowered into the grave. My legs felt weak and I sank to the ground sobbing. People gathered round to help me up, but I didn't want to get up. I wanted to sink into the earth.

It was my mother who forced me to look up. She lifted my chin and told me to open my eyes, and there was the most stunning rainbow I have ever seen. The colours were vivid, bright and intense and the more I looked at it, the more the colours sparkled. The rainbow was so lovely I knew it was Charlotte speaking to me. I got up and looked over at the street that ran past the cemetery. People were stopping their cars and getting out of them to gaze at the rainbow. I've never seen a rainbow so intense and colourful since.

The world stood still for me in that moment and colour came back into my life again. I hugged my two other children and told them that wherever we were in the world Charlotte would be with us, smiling down on us, reminding us that you can see rainbows anywhere.

For Ruby in this story, a simple rainbow instantly transformed her grief. Of course, as is always the case, some people might interpret this story as chance, but any person who has lost a loved one knows differently. Angels pour comfort into grieving hearts by revealing themselves in ordinary but extraordinary ways. In this way, without causing alarm or distress, they can show you clearly and personally that you are not alone and that those you have lost are here with you right now, in every moment of your life, in every bit of creation.

Remember what I said about angels appearing in the most unexpected of places? Well, Maya found her angel in a swimming pool!

When Kai was born everybody said that he had been kissed by an angel because the groove above his lip is so deep. It made him look adorable. Anyway, fast-forward to his ninth birthday. I'd organised a private swimming party for him and five of his friends at the health club I worked at. It was one of the perks of the job being able to book the pool for an hour without anyone else there. Everything was going great when suddenly the boys started shouting at me. Kai had been practising his handstands in the pool and had knocked his head.

I leapt into the pool, dived under the water and pulled him to the surface. Then I dragged him to the side of the pool. I shouted at one of the boys to call 999 and tried to revive him. He was not responding and then I don't know what happened, but I kind of froze in panic. I couldn't move. The boys were shouting at me and Kai was just lying there in front of me.

How I wished I had read my first aid manuals more closely. I didn't know what I should be doing and there were no swimming staff on hand to help out. I cursed myself for organising the party and not thinking about safety.

And then a miracle happened. Kai started to cough, and a shower of water squirted onto my face. Soon he was up on his feet. The ambulance crew arrived, checked him over and he was fine.

The next morning, I asked him if he remembered anything from when he hit his head until the time he woke up. He told me that he remembered me kissing him, but there was another woman there with light darting out of her forehead kissing him too, and he didn't know who she was. She had to be his guardian angel, don't you think?

Leo spent two weeks in intensive care, following a serious infection.

It is only now that I realise just how seriously poorly I was. My doctor told me it was touch and go. I don't remember much about my time in intensive care as I was unconscious for most of it but there is one striking memory. It was around midnight and I was wide awake. I was not dreaming. I felt this warm glow rush over me. It was like a tide, starting with my toes and then rushing to me head. There was a shining light too. It was so bright I had to squint and then cover my eyes. I had absolutely no fear throughout this light experience, just peace and comfort from the inside out and the outside in. I also knew that I was out of danger and I was going to recover.

The next morning when the doctors checked me out they were amazed. The infection had cleared overnight.

Kim experienced a similar comfort and peace from the inside out.

We lost my mom to cancer a year before my son Oliver was born. I had never felt her loss so badly and so wished that she was around to share him with us. When Oliver was three months old he had to have a hernia operation, which everyone except me considered to be a minor procedure. I was worried sick.

The operation went all to plan, just lots of waiting around and worrying. He was in and out of theatre within an hour and I was so relieved when we went to fetch him back from the recovery room.

We stayed at the hospital for a further few hours to make sure he was fine and when the time came to leave, my partner went to fetch the car. Only Oliver, who was in his pram, and I were in the corridor. Suddenly, I felt what I can only describe as a huge 'cape of warmth' wrapped around my shoulders. It made me feel protected and safe. It gave me the feeling that I knew from now on Oliver would be fine and watched over. I'm sure that Mom was sending us a message and putting her arms around us both to give us a big warm hug and say that everything was okay now, which is exactly what she would have done had she been around. It was a truly amazing experience.

Here's a story I find myself returning to time and time again.

My mother used to be a nurse and she had seen many dead bodies in her time. She would often tell me that she never wanted me to see her like that. When she died, she wanted me to remember her alive and full of vitality and didn't wish me to see her body when she had gone. So, when her time came and the hospital called to say she had died suddenly in the night, they asked me if I wanted to see her one more time. I immediately said no.

In the days before the funeral I was under a lot of pressure from friends and family to say my goodbyes. They were all very well-meaning and were trying to ease my grief. My husband told me that he had visited his father after he had died, and it had been incredibly healing for him. I told him that although that may have worked for him, it wasn't right for me. Everyone told me that I would regret it, but I had made up my mind.

I was firm in my decision right up until an hour or so before the funeral, when I started to waver for the first time. A part of me wanted to hold Mum one more time, to kiss her and say goodbye. I thought of Mum lying alone in her coffin. Perhaps she needed to be held as much as I longed to hold her. Perhaps I was wrong, and everyone was right? Perhaps I needed closure?

I was sitting there feeling wretched when I felt this gust of air on my cheek. It was so refreshing, and it gave me a feeling of strength and clarity. My bedroom door was closed and there were no windows open. Don't ask me how I knew, but I just sensed my mother was close by. I wiped away my tears and got ready for the funeral.

I thought only of the laughter and the happy times I had shared with Mum during the funeral. As her coffin disappeared behind the heavy curtains and I said my last goodbyes, I felt a kiss on first my right cheek and then my left cheek. In my mind's eye I clearly saw Mum smiling and dancing, just the way she wanted me to remember her. From now on, every time I think of her, I see an image of her as for ever alive, vibrant, laughing and smiling.

ANGELIC CONTAGION

Simply reading or hearing true angel stories has a calming, healing effect and that's why I included this selection here. As you read these stories, you may have felt strangely comforted or just better about your life in some way. You may well have felt encouraged to be kinder and more compassionate to others too.

In this way every angel story that is experienced, read, told and shared has a ripple effect. It works one story, one person at a time, transforming the world with its love and light, like an angelic contagion. And it all started when someone – and that person could be you – felt, read, saw or heard the word 'angel' in the sense it should be experienced – as a reminder that this world is not as it seems. That there is an unshakable force of love and goodness both out there and within you and there is no point gaining the world if you lose sight of that force.

Hopefully, what you've read so far has helped flood your mind and heart with angel inspirations so that they become your first, last and every thought and feeling. Next, you'll learn how to see, hear and sense angels, so that they are no longer something you deliberately think, hear or read about other people experiencing. They are who you truly are.

PART TWO

The Secret Language of Angels

'When hearts listen, angels sing.'

ANONYMOUS

CHAPTER FOUR

How to See Angels

To start truly seeing, hearing and feeling angels everywhere, the only essential requirement is *you*.

You don't need to meditate for hours or visit psychics or mediums, or sign up to workshops, courses and products. Sure, visit an expert every now and then. But beware of dependency. Chapter Nine (and the 'Guidelines for Visiting Mediums and Lightworkers' at the back of the book) will help you identify a true healer who has your best interests at heart, but for now just bear in mind that however 'gifted' a channel claims to be, however much comfort or insight a psychic brings from the other side, they are *not* the true and permanent authority on your angels or the real way to connect to them.

You are.

And you don't need to have a full-blown, dramatic angelic vision, either. Although science has shown that paranormal experiences that defy rational explanation can and do happen, in all the research I have done collating angel stories, I see that dramatic visions are no more or less healing than subtle ones.

The suggestions for angel-attracting rituals coming up are not written in stone and you are encouraged to personalise them. I am just presenting them as guidelines that have worked for me, to get you thinking along the right lines.

SACRED TIMES

A quick word about rituals before we begin.

First, don't be alarmed by the word 'ritual'. As with the word 'angel', there is no religious or pagan association (unless you want to create one). Rituals are simply repeatable actions – things you *do* – performed with mindful intention – understanding of their significance. Rituals give our lives meaning. They bring an element of the sacred into our lives, or, if you prefer, an awareness of something higher or greater within ourselves.

I love rituals because the focus is on being proactive, taking meaningful and positive action. You may have come across the idea that intention, or the power of positive thinking, is everything when it comes to attracting angels. It does make some sense – thoughts are energy – but for me it can be unhelpful. I fiercely advocate the power of positive actions *alongside* positive thinking. I've seen many people get trapped in their heads, their focus entirely on thoughts and affirmations, which can cripple their ability to get out there and actually *do* something positive with their lives.

It's not all about your thinking, and when things don't go well it isn't just because you haven't zapped all that negative thinking!

Obviously, if you don't believe in yourself or that something can happen, you decrease your chances of success. And if you don't believe in angels you won't be as receptive to them.

But your thoughts are not entirely to blame.

Just as we eventually learn to trust a person by their actions and not their words, perhaps the same applies to attracting angels. What if angels respond not just to our thoughts and intentions but also to our actions? What we actually do. What if your daily actions signal to spirit that you really are someone worth trusting and investing in? What if your daily actions are the *real* secret?

What if angels are more attracted to supporting someone whose actions match their intentions? Seen in this clear light, when it comes to your angels you are not just what you *think* you are, but also what you repeatedly *do*. Doing something with mindful understanding of why you are doing it is where the power of your thoughts really comes in. Repeat an action often enough and it becomes a habit; but habits can't ignite change because they are mindless. They lack personal meaning. For actions to create lasting change they need to be filled to the brim with meaning. They need to be *ritualised*.

Research[36] backs up the life-changing power of rituals. Numerous studies show that your brain can be led by your daily actions as well as your thoughts. Positive change starts with what you repeatedly do – your small everyday actions – regardless of what you are thinking. If you've ever felt your mood boosted after a brisk walk, you will already know the truth of this. It's how rituals work. The power lies in actually doing them and how they can focus your concentration on the present moment and the reason for your actions.

EVERYDAY RITUALS

Simple daily rituals are all that you need to attract angels. The transformative impact comes from repeating them. Intention is helpful but, intriguingly, research[37] shows that you don't need to believe in the power of a ritual for it to work. The ritual just needs to have personal meaning for you, so you understand the reason you are repeatedly doing it. And the reason here is clear and simple: each ritual is something you can do that brings your angels closer to you.

Don't worry if you don't yet believe that daily rituals work. Simply do them and let them prove their ability to attract angels. Above all, let rituals teach you the ultimate angel hack, which is that the path to joy is in your own hands. Fulfilment can't be found outside yourself in relationships, popularity, money, career or status. It can only be found in what you choose to do every day.

And now you are more aware of the power of your actions, you can approach your daily angel-attracting rituals with the mindful reverence they deserve.

TAKE 21

Each day that you incorporate these positive actions – rituals – into your life increases your chances of seeing angels, but you won't likely find they are working until you've been doing them for at least three weeks. This is the period of time that research[38] suggests it takes for neuropathways to form in your brain and for there to be a noticeable change in how you think, feel and act. So, you also need to practise the angelic arts of discipline and patience!

Your conscious mind (ego) doesn't like to be told something is for life. It is likely to rebel. So, to keep your conscious mind on your side, you need to tell yourself you will do these rituals for just a few weeks and then you will reassess. Commit yourself initially to a minimum of twenty-one days and then hopefully, when those three weeks are up, the uplifting glimpses you start to catch of angels will motivate you to commit to doing them in the long term. You will have convinced your conscious mind this is really worth it!

WHAT'S YOUR CHANNEL?

Now that you are beginning to fully understand the science of rituals and why you need to keep repeating them, it's time to select your favourite angel channel. No, it's not Netflix! Channelling is the term used to describe communication between yourself and your angels. You have the potential to channel through seeing, hearing, thinking, feeling and dreaming. It's often the case that we find ourselves more attracted to a particular one of these channels, so over the next few days start observing yourself objectively. Find out more about yourself.

- Do you think in pictures or words?
- Do you sense and feel life deeply?
- Are you a good listener?
- Do you trust your gut, your intuition?

This chapter focuses on rituals to help you see angels; the next chapter offers rituals to help you hear them and the chapter after that explores ways to feel them. As you are encouraged to do your ritual work for twenty-one days, you can choose to focus your attention on seeing for a week, then hearing for the week after and then feeling in the final week, to see what resonates most. Or you can perform all the rituals in each of the three chapters each day.

I'm hoping that in the coming weeks you might notice a primary channel that feels natural to you. If that's the case, you may want to focus your attention there initially or you may wish to work on opening up all channels. Whatever you decide, play to your strengths and don't try to force anything, as the best state of mind in which to connect to angels is a relaxed one.

Let's start with what most of us think we want – to actually see angels. There's a psychic term for that: clairvoyance.

Clairvoyance means 'clear seeing'. Visions of spirits and seeing angels with our eyes wide open can happen on rare occasions, but it's far more likely for you to see angels in other ways. As these other ways typically seem 'normal' or familiar, you may not have recognised them for the angel visions they truly are. Let's open your eyes.

- Vivid, realistic and memorable night-time dreams are perhaps the most common way to see angels. Indeed, I believe dreams may be angels' preferred way to show themselves.
- You may 'see' images with your internal vision or mind's eye, like watching a movie on a projector screen in your mind. This can happen with your eyes open, but it is most likely to happen when you are awake with closed eyes.

- You may have a vision of something happening in your present (or future) that you cannot possibly have knowledge of. For example, you 'see' a loved one saying or doing something, and this later turns out to be accurate. (Clairvoyance can often merge with intuition and precognition, which are discussed in Chapter Six.)
- You may notice an unexplained orb of light in a photograph. You could send it for expert analysis to see if there is another explanation, such as dust specks or light flares, but in many ways that does not matter. It's the sense of magical possibility that looking at the orb inspires that's important.
- You may see lights or mists of many colours – perhaps a spark of light in the corner of your eye, which you might dismiss as static or your imagination.
- You may look up and see in the clouds the shape of wings, feathers or other meaningful symbols in the sky.
- You could be inexplicably mesmerised by an image, photo, painting, statue or post.
- You pick up a book or a magazine at random, or scroll on your phone, and the words you read feel personal or deeply insightful, somehow meant just for you. This can happen with videos and TV, too.
- Signs in the 'real world' may offer you a sense of comfort or make you feel there is more to life than meets the eye. These signs can be anything and they are deeply personal and therefore variable, but some of the most common include feathers, birds, rainbows, butterflies, coins, numbers and objects lost and found.

- You may sometimes catch a glimpse of someone or something, but when you focus and look properly you can't see anything.
- You observe others' acts of kindness and compassion. For example, you watch a teenager giving up their seat for someone older and for reasons you can't explain, this act inspires you to be kinder yourself. Reading about or watching true-life stories about selfless acts of courage has a similar impact.
- You watch a movie, a video or a TV show and it inspires and motivates you, making you feel good about being a human being.
- Someone is kind or goes out of their way to help or make your life easier, for no reason and with no expectation in return. For example, they give you their parking ticket that still has a few hours left.
- After spending time with someone – and that someone could be a loved one, a stranger or even a pet or animal – you just feel better.
- When someone thanks or appreciates you, you can see in their eyes, or in their words if they message you, that their gratitude and appreciation is sincere.
- You may often lose track of time and feel a deep sense of awe when you encounter visual beauty in art, nature or life.

ANGEL EYES

You may be familiar with a movie called *127 Hours*, starring James Franco. The film tells the true story of Aron Lee Ralston (born 1975), an American outdoorsman, engineer and motivational speaker who survived a canyoneering accident by cutting off his own arm. Literally stuck between a rock and a hard place and feeling his life ebbing away, he had a vision of a young boy playing. He knew that this was his future son – and this gave him the strength to amputate his arm. A few years later he got married and had a son – the son he had seen in his vision.

This is a vivid and powerful example of the phenomenon of angel eyes. Over the years I have had countless stories sent to me by people who see the world this way.

Here's Lena's enlightening experience.

I lost my mother last year. I never got a chance to say goodbye. Her death was sudden and unexpected, and I miss her in every heartbeat. My pain was doubled because I was pregnant at the time and three weeks after my mother died, I miscarried a baby girl. It was the darkest and loneliest time in my life. I'm still hurting and probably always will, but four months after the loss of my unborn daughter I woke up in the middle of the night. I was sure I heard the female voice of a child calling me by my name – but it was my middle name, Mary, not my first name. This is significant as, a few years before she died, my mother had started to call me Mary more often than she used my first name. It may have been because I often told her that I loved that name.

Anyway, I sat up and saw in front of me on the wall the name Mary in lights. It was like someone had projected it there. I rubbed my eyes and looked around the room. The light was not coming from anything or anyone. My husband was sound asleep by my side and my dog in his basket, snoring. My name stayed up there in lights for a few minutes and then it slowly started to fade. I watched it fade and then, when the light had completely gone, I felt a surge of hope and love. I knew my unborn child was with my mother in spirit and my angels were sending me my name in lights to let me know they believed in me and always would be there for me.

Angels often appear to comfort the dying when their time approaches, as Noah describes below.

A few days before my grandfather died, he told me there was an angel called Daniel beside him. I didn't pay much attention, as he was suffering from severe cognitive decline. He had no idea who I was any more, and he didn't even look at me when I came into the room. It was heartbreaking, as my father had died when I was ten, so my grandfather had stepped in and taken on the role of my dad.

The day before my grandfather died, I went to visit as usual, but this time was different. He knew who I was and for about twenty minutes we had the most beautiful conversation. I was able to tell him how much I loved him, and he told me the same. He also told me that Daniel was his guardian angel who was going to make sure he was okay. Daniel would make sure he was not alone when the moment came. He even pointed to the end of his bed as if expecting me to see Daniel, too. I saw nothing. Then he drifted away again and didn't know who I was any more.

I left the room in tears that day. I think I sensed that this was the last time I would speak to my grandfather and I was right. I got a call in the night saying he had passed. When I went in the next morning, I talked to the night nurse who had been with him and he said it had been a peaceful death. He was holding his hand as he passed. I told the nurse about the angel, Daniel, and the nurse laughed. He told me his name was Daniel, but he also said he believed my grandfather. He said he often saw unexplained lights surrounding patients.

Now I don't know whether my grandfather actually saw his guardian angel, or whether his guardian angel was really his human nurse, Daniel. It doesn't really matter. All I do know is that when he passed, there was an angel present, holding his hand.

By contrast, Amir's angels appeared to him through dreams and flowers.

We had only been married for eighteen months when my wife Yasmin died in a car crash. She was thirty. One minute she was rushing to say goodbye to me as she headed to work. The next she was gone, and she took my heart and my future with her. I missed her with body, mind and soul.

One night I had a dream that saved me. It didn't seem like a dream as it felt so real. In the dream I was sitting down, and a girl was speaking to me. I didn't know her, but she was dressed in white and had long white gloves on. She told me her name was Lily.

When I woke up, I had no immediate memory of the dream. But I do remember that I didn't wake up choking with tears, as I had been doing ever since my wife had died. This was unusual in itself, because that day I was meeting my wife's parents to discuss the funeral arrangements. When we talked about the choice of flowers, I said I didn't want traditional flowers as I preferred something bright and vibrant to celebrate my wife's sunny personality. But then my mother-in-law said something that brought my dream right back into my mind. She said, 'Are you sure? Lilies are so beautiful and in flower language they mean "life after death". I think we should have lilies.'

Throughout the funeral I stared at the lilies resting on my wife's coffin. For the first and not the last time since my wife died, I felt her presence all around me. I continue to feel it ever since. I will never stop missing my wife but, all these years later, whenever I think of her it is with a smile before a tear because I know she has not gone. I know that because an angel spoke to me in a dream, and I will never forget that lilies represent life after death.

Many pet owners will be able to relate to this story, sent in by Rona.

Times have not been easy for me. I live alone and last week my dog – my best friend – died. Unless you are a dog owner yourself, you won't understand how these fur angels walk into our hearts every day. One night, I asked for a sign, anything that would help me feel less alone. The next morning, I woke up to find two beautiful white feathers exactly in the spot in my kitchen where I used to feed my dog every morning. They were lying side by side and were perfect. I have no idea how they got there, as the windows were closed. I can't describe the comfort that these feathers appearing gave me. It was not a coincidence. It was a sign and I'll never forget it.

Angels can appear in the most unexpected places, as Oscar relates.

Every weekday for about a year, I would get off the train on my way home from work and walk past an elderly lady. She would be sitting on a bench just beside the station exit in her bright blue coat. I don't know why she sat there. Perhaps she was waiting for someone to pick her up or perhaps it was her daily routine to take a rest there. For no reason at all, she would always give me the broadest smile and sometimes wave, too. It wasn't just me. She did this for everyone that passed by. She smiled and waved for no apparent reason.

At first, I simply thought she was eccentric, and I ignored her. But over time I started to smile in return and, when I wasn't carrying too many bags, I would wave back. It felt strangely comforting. We never spoke, but it was only when she wasn't there any more that I realised how much I missed her smile. It was a gift of joy she gave me that was priceless. I think of her often and wonder if she was my guardian angel because she taught me so much without saying anything. Since she's been gone, I try to smile for no reason, just like she did.

All these people saw things clearly, whether with their eyes open or closed. Their extraordinary visions comforted them beyond words, as only angelic visions can. I longed for decades to see beings of light flying around with my eyes open. I truly don't have that longing any more. I don't need to see anything outside myself. I see angels through my dreams and through mental images. I use my inner eyes. I also look for angels expressing themselves in the world around me, through nature, art or other people.

If you tend to think in pictures or notice how things look rather than how they sound, feel, taste or smell, you may be particularly sensitive to developing clairvoyance. The following clear-seeing rituals can help you fine-tune that gift. Perform them daily for at least the next twenty-one days. And even if you don't think of yourself as a visual person, you can still benefit greatly from a week of focusing on developing your inner vision. Opening up all possible channels of communication gives your angels more options to show themselves to and through you.

CLEAR-SEEING RITUALS

Enter the twilight zone: Twice a day you have an incredible opportunity to see angels. That's immediately on waking and just before you go to sleep. Those twilight moments between waking and sleeping or sleeping and waking are sacred because your brain enters a highly receptive state of theta brainwaves, which occur most often in sleep or in states of relaxation and deep meditation. And once you become aware of how powerful these moments in your day are, you can use them to reprogramme negative beliefs. As you drift off to sleep, and then again when you wake up, simply flood your mind with images of angels comforting you.

Step outside: Continuing the twilight zone theme on waking spend a few moments visualising yourself living the day awaiting you in a way your better angels would approve. And just before you go to sleep take this observational stance one step further. Review your day from the perspective of your better angels. Step outside yourself, detach yourself from your thoughts and feelings and observe and what you did in your day through the lens of your guardian angel. Or if you prefer, observe your daily actions from the perspective of someone who loves you very much, your best friend, for example. The idea is to encourage you to detach from identification with the material, your thoughts and feelings and to connect to the part of you which is eternal, your soul or your better angels.

Your daily daydream: There's always at least one moment in a day when your mind is free to daydream. During these times your conscious mind is preoccupied with keeping your body on track as it performs a repetitive task such as showering or walking, offering your unconscious, the place where your angels like to meet you, an opportunity to take centre stage. Savour any opportunity you get to simply daydream and visualise uplifting pictures, images and symbols.

A whole new world: Chances are you only notice what you think is relevant – but take your blinkers off. Look at the leaves on the trees or on the ground, observe buildings when you walk and notice what people are wearing when you talk to them. Notice what you didn't notice before.

See the signs: Pay attention when you notice a sign that has personal meaning to you, such as an unexpected white feather, a rainbow, a robin or whatever feels magical crossing your path.

Stop, take a deep breath and thank your angels for letting you know they are right there walking beside you.

Cloud-watching: Remember when you were a child and you lay in the grass watching the clouds shift shape above you? If you don't, create a memory right now. Find somewhere safe to lie, sit or stand and watch the magical shapes the clouds form in the sky. Don't stare intently at them, just gaze gently. Be sure to avoid looking directly at the sun.

Meet the sun and the stars: Admire a glorious sunset or sunrise or take up stargazing, which is a mesmerising way to develop your clairvoyant ability. Indeed, admiring the wonder of any natural scene, such as a shimmering lake or a flock of birds forming a perfect arrow, is ideal training for your inner eye.

Fairy tales: The language of clairvoyance is symbols and images. When you were a child you likely loved fairy tales and the stories you liked the most would probably have had wonderful illustrations. Find a fully illustrated fairy-tale book. As you look at it again with adult eyes, notice feelings inside you, both familiar and unfamiliar ones. This is a positive sign, as it shows that you are starting to kick-start your imagination, which is your direct path to clairvoyance.

Step inside: A more advanced picture technique is to choose a painting or photograph that captures your imagination and study it. Then close your eyes and try to remember it. See the picture in your mind's eye. Next, imagine yourself stepping into that picture. Spend time exploring the world there. After a while you may want to open your eyes to look at the picture again to refresh your memory before 'stepping' back into it.

Candle in the wind: Find a candle and light it. Stare gently – not directly – into the flames for a minute. Then snuff out the candle and close your eyes. Can you see the image of the flame on your eyelids? Watch that image until it fades. Then, reimagine it or create another picture to see with your inner eye. Angel images can sometimes appear to us if we do this exercise.

Mind shapes: Draw a large letter 'I' and a large 'Y' close to each other on a piece of paper. Look at both letters and then cover up the 'Y' shape with your hand and look only at the 'I'. In your mind's eye, let the 'I' transform itself into a 'Y'. See the line of the 'arm' dividing and turning outwards. Try it again, only this time try to see one arm of the 'Y' growing faster than the other. Do it again and visualise one arm waiting for the other to complete before it moves. Imagine in your mind's eye one of the arms moving and, when it stops, see the other moving.

Keep a dream journal: Recalling your dreams helps you to think in images and stimulates your clairvoyant ability.

Light someone up: Consciously try to help or inspire someone else on a daily basis. That someone could be a loved one or it could be a stranger; it doesn't matter – just notice how your words or actions can light someone else up. It could be as simple as holding a door open with a warm smile for the person walking behind you, or making a cup of coffee or tea for a loved one without being asked. Just be an angel and do something kind for someone else.

A chapter a day: Research has shown that reading can connect you to your inner angel in that it makes you more compassionate and likely to be kind. Read for half an hour before you go to bed (or listen to audiobooks if you prefer).[39] In the Resources section (see page 218), you'll find some suggested spiritual reading.

But don't restrict yourself to non-fiction; fiction can also ignite your empathy, creativity, curiosity and sense of possibility. There are suggestions for fiction in the Resources section too.

Open your third eye: According to some ancient traditions there is an energy centre associated with clairvoyance just above the area between your eyes, called the third eye chakra. Whether that is true or not it's a beautiful idea. Every day gently rub that area to release any tension. As you do so, imagine you have a third eye there. It is now wide open, noticing not only what is seen but also what is unseen. And during the day, if you feel overwhelmed, imagine your third eye closing.

Note: If you feel spaced out after performing any of these angel rituals, be sure to drink a glass of water, stretch and yawn. Or go for a brisk walk, have a light snack or do anything that will ground you.

If you feel sceptical or maybe you can't see anything at all, just keep practising daily. Give it time.

These sorts of roadblocks are a part of spiritual growth and much of your own personal growth depends on how you deal with them. So, the idea is not to steer clear of them completely but to become aware of them, understand why you have them and then to find ways to ensure they don't interfere with your growth.

When you hit a block or a barrier, try to let go of any expectations you may have of how angels should show themselves to you. Angelic helpers see the bigger picture rather than the smaller details of your life, so you may not see what you expect. Doubt is another barrier, but just because you see something inside your head does not mean it is not real.

If fear of seeing something frightening is holding you back, please remember that everything that comes from angels is loving and positive and so if it is frightening, it is coming from your ego, not your heart or your angels. And remember you are always the one in charge of what you see. If you approach your clairvoyance training with an attitude of love for the purposes of healing yourself and others, you can't go wrong.

Another roadblock orchestrated by your ego is trying too hard. When you try too hard the message you send your angels is that you don't trust them to be there for you. And if you don't trust your angels, it's harder for them to break through.

Lack of self-belief is another huge spiritual roadblock. You don't have to be perfect to see angels. As long as you learn and grow from your mistakes, angels will support you every step of the way. We all doubt ourselves from time to time. Researchers call this imposter syndrome and many highly successful people experience it, so you are in fine company. If you doubt yourself, try to see yourself as your guardian angel – your best friend – would.

If the people in your life have negative views about you or your belief in the world of spirit, remember that no one makes you feel or believe something without your consent. *You* are in charge of your thoughts and feelings. A good place to start would be to avoid people and situations that don't support you. If you encounter criticism see if there is anything you can learn from it rather than closing your mind. Protect yourself. Keep boundaries. Helping others selflessly as recommended in the 'light someone up' ritual (see page 85) is admirable, but not if it diminishes you. You can't give to others if you don't give to yourself first. And if you can't avoid negative people and situations, visualise white or golden light or the arms of an angel folding around you, forming a protective bubble, until you can get out of the situation.

Self-care is the absolute rock of spiritual growth. Never underestimate the importance of taking good care of your physical health by eating and sleeping well, and exercising regularly, preferably in the fresh air, as this will make you a clearer channel. Your body is the temple for your soul. Treat it with the reverence and respect it deserves.

LOOK INSIDE

Taking care of yourself also means taking care of your thoughts. Although I gave positive actions pride of place earlier and expressed my reservations about the positive-thinking mantra, thinking is unavoidable. So why not think in a way that is going to increase the likelihood of angels revealing themselves to you?

Tell yourself that you are creative and can see angels. Ditch the negative soundtrack. Is your perspective one of curiosity and infinite possibility or are you wearing a blindfold?

Parables can create memorable images to explain spiritual concepts. Here's one of my favourite ones, about the life-enhancing power of perspective. You might wish to mull it over, especially if negative thoughts are dimming your light. You always have the power to choose your thoughts, change your perspective and see your light. Which baby are you in this parable?

A Tale of Two Babies

There were two babies in a mother's womb. One twin asked the other twin if they believed in life after delivery. The other replied in the affirmative and, bursting with excitement, suggested they prepare themselves for what was out there for them. There might be light instead of darkness and they might even be able to walk and eat themselves.

The twin who'd asked this question was not convinced and told the other twin off for believing in fairy tales. After all, it was clear that the umbilical cord was the source of their nutrition and, if there was life after delivery, the umbilical cord wasn't long enough to sustain them.

The other twin grew silent. After all there was no proof and it was true that the umbilical cord really wasn't long enough. But then the twin wondered out loud if perhaps life was different on the outside. The other shot down this hope by reminding them both that delivery would be the end of life as they knew it and after delivery there was nothing but darkness. Also, nobody had ever come back from the outside to prove to them it was real.

The hopeful twin felt a surge of strength from the inside out and talked about someone called Mother and how she would take care of them. The doubtful twin screamed in anguish at this belief. Nobody had ever seen this Mother.

Another fairy tale. But the hopeful twin refused to be silent and proclaimed that Mother was all around them and in them. They lived. Without her they would not exist in their dark world.

The doubtful twin doubled down, asserting that they couldn't see her, so it was only logical that she did not exist. At this point the other spoke with a calm confidence that surprised them both. The hopeful twin stated that when they were silent, they could hear and sense her. There was a reality out there, and quietly imagining that reality, seeing it, believing it in their heart was the only way to give their life on the inside any meaning.

Neither twin knows the truth for sure, but one chooses to be open whereas the other shuts down the possibility of something more.

SHOW YOURSELF

In the words of psychiatrist Carl Jung, '*Your vision will become clear only when you look inside your heart. Who looks inside, awakens . . .*'

Don't waste another precious moment. Start seeing angels and all the beautiful things you associate with them as often as you can. To boost your clairvoyance, aim to *think in pictures* rather than words. Paint your own angels with your inner eye. The more you look inside and visualise angels, the more you give your thoughts – and the images you create with those thoughts

– wings. Then, in no time at all, your inner angel will awaken, and you will start seeing angels everywhere.

Seeing from the inside out is a stunning way to connect to the invisible world, but don't think it is the only way. One of the most exciting things I have learned about angels is that once they capture your attention, they find more and more wonderful ways to show themselves. There are so many astonishing things, just waiting for you to notice them.

CHAPTER FIVE

How to Hear Angels

I know that hearing voices is often said to be the first sign of madness. Yes, it may sound a little crazy. I used to think that too, but today I am convinced that angelic voices are anything but crazy. They might just be the sanest voices you ever hear.

The psychic term used for hearing voices is clairaudience, meaning 'clear hearing'. It is receiving comfort, guidance and inspiration through sound. It is hearing or tuning into voices, sounds or music from spirit and hearing those vibrations inside and outside your head as clearly as if someone is talking to you.

One of my objectives in writing this book is to normalise conversation about the paranormal and show that experiences many of us consider paranormal or extraordinary are, in fact, ordinary. From the outset I'm going to make it crystal clear that angelic voices are completely different from the voices associated with psychiatric problems. The former are calming, coherent, positive and harm no one, whereas the latter are potentially chaotic, incoherent, negative and harmful. As you can see from the examples of angel talk below, you may well have already experienced some of them, but dismissed them at the time as imagination or meaningless.

- You hear a disembodied voice say something profound or life-changing to you. The voice may also give you directions or tell you where to find a lost item. Typically, the voice is familiar because it belongs to a deceased relative or a loved one, and you hear it in your head, in your dreams or, on rare occasions, outside your head. Sometimes the voice is your own and sometimes it is not familiar but simply clear and decisive.
- You wake up and, before you open your eyes, you hear someone calling your name, even though no one did so. You may also experience this in a crowd of people or when walking in the street, but when you turn or look around for the source, there isn't one.
- You turn on the TV or radio or go online and hear exactly the thing you need to be hearing. Similarly, you may overhear someone else's conversation, and what they say speaks directly to your heart and spirit or to a situation you are currently experiencing.
- You can't get a song or a piece of music out of your head, and when you turn on the radio or TV or go online you hear it again. Similarly, you may hear a song or a piece of music that has special significance for you or a departed loved one, played at the perfect time to bring you comfort.
- You hear snatches of beautiful music you haven't heard before, which have no detectable source.
- You have a deep appreciation for music, and lose track of time when listening to music you love.

- You can sometimes hear the whispers of departed loved ones or their voices expressed in the sound of birdsong, waves lapping on the shore, the howling of the wind or the sighing of the breeze.
- Your doorbell or phone rings, but when you respond you find there is no one there – you just know it is a loved one in spirit calling out to you.
- You may hear sounds typically associated with a departed loved one, for example coins jangling in a pocket or heels tapping on the floor.
- You experience a sharp, high-pitched ringing sound in your ear for a few moments. This is not the same as the long-term harsh noise associated with tinnitus. Some angel experts believe this gentle ringing comes from the other side, as if heaven is downloading information for your soul. This may or may not be the case, but now you know there might be an association, so if this happens, take a moment to let the divine wisdom sink in and work its magic on an unconscious level.
- You find yourself hungry for knowledge, eager to learn new things. You have so many questions whirling in your mind.
- Someone is speaking to you and you find yourself listening intently, without interrupting, because what they are saying resonates deeply with you.
- You hear yourself saying something profound to yourself or out loud to another person and you have no idea where the sudden inspiration came from. Similarly, you are tempted to say something that isn't true or in line with your values and integrity, but something stops you and you speak honestly instead.

LISTEN TO ME

Earlier I talked about how I believe the voice of my mother in spirit may well have saved my life when I was at a junction deciding whether to turn right or left (see page 20). The voice sounded like it was coming from outside my head. At the time it felt like a miracle, but in the years that followed I seriously doubted it and wondered if it was simply a memory from my past resurfacing, because my mother would often tell me to take the right path, meaning personal choice rather than an actual path. However, over time and as stories started to flood in from readers reporting similar unexplained voices or sounds that healed, comforted or even saved their lives, I knew my experience was not an isolated one. I also discovered this phenomenon is reported in the media from time to time.

One remarkable story that was well reported at the time happened during the 9/11 attacks on the World Trade Center in New York. Ron DiFrancesco, a trader, was on the 84th floor of the second tower when the second hijacked plane smashed into the 81st floor. Everyone on his floor scrambled to the staircases, but he froze with panic and lay down on the floor with his eyes closed, unable to move. Then he heard an invisible but insistent male voice urging him to get up and head to safety. The voice gave him the courage he needed, and he was the last person to leave the tower before it collapsed. He believed an angel spoke to him and rescued him.

Another account of a famous disembodied voice dates back to 1983, when explorer and scientist James Sevigny fell thousands of feet down a mountain in the Canadian Rockies, breaking several bones. He curled up in pain, expecting to die, but instead heard a female voice urging him to get up and make it back to the campsite. It took him several years to come forward and tell his story.

Similar stories have been sent to me over the years. Some of them are just as dramatic, but most instances of clairaudience are more subtle. This does not make them any the less profound and potentially life-changing for the person experiencing them. Quite the opposite: they feel miraculous in their impact.

This happened to me in 2008. I often find myself returning to it and wondering if I imagined it. My younger sister died in 1999 following an unexpected blood clot. I was very close to her and have never got over the loss. It was especially tough when I had my first child in 2007 and post-natal depression struck. On the evening of 19 April 2008, I fell asleep exhausted. At 2.22 a.m. I woke up. Someone was calling my name. I knew the time because I checked my watch. I wasn't afraid. I thought it might be my partner, but he was asleep beside me. Then, I heard my name again.

The voice was my sister's. I couldn't see anything, I just heard her. She told me that I was going to be okay and I was a great mom because when we were growing up, I had been like a mom to her. She told me she loved me. Nothing in life was meant to be easy and she was always there for me if I wanted to talk to her. She then told me my baby was going to wake up in a few minutes and it was time for her to go. I begged her not to go, but as soon as I started talking to her there was only silence. I sat there in the silence for a few minutes missing her, but also feeling happy for the first time in months. As my sister predicted, within five minutes my baby started crying. That familiar knot of dread in my stomach when I heard the crying had gone. It never came back.

The conversation with my sister felt like she had been sitting on the end of my bed, chatting to me as she used to do. It felt like it had always been when she was alive. It was utterly incredible. I didn't used to think much about an afterlife and if asked would likely have said I didn't think it was real. I don't just think it is real now, I know it is.

It is easy to dismiss stories like the one above from Jaysha as recollections of the voice of a departed loved one – for many years that is what I told myself about hearing my mother's voice when I believe she saved my life. But this does not explain away stories where voices from the other side offer advice or a warning that applies very much to the present moment.

I was driving my usual route to work. I'd been doing this for eighteen months and was probably on autopilot. I knew the best route, what was coming up and which lane was best to drive in. But this day, for reasons I can't explain, I heard this voice. It sounded like my own or it could have been my mother's voice. People often said we sounded similar. This voice told me to change lanes now. I did not question it and, as soon as I was in the other lane, huge pieces of plaster and wood fell out of the truck I had been behind. The material smashed onto the road where I would have been driving. I drove past it feeling incredibly grateful and relieved for the near miss. I'm not sure if this was my sixth sense kicking in, if it was an angel or if it was just random. But it felt anything but random. It felt like I was meant to hear that voice.

Paz in the story above heard the voice of an angel telling her to change lanes when she least expected it. This 'not-what-I-expected-to-happen' theme is one that runs through many of the stories sent to me. It does seem that trying too hard has the opposite effect and may explain why a lot of auditory experiences happen to people when they are driving, walking, doing chores or other repetitive tasks, or when they are in the twilight stage between waking and falling asleep. They are in a relaxed, almost meditative state, which is most conducive to these kinds of experiences.

It is not just through a voice or words that angels speak. I have lost count of the number of messages about how natural sounds, such as rain falling or a waterfall, can comfort and heal. And if you hear a song repeatedly in your head or on the radio, it could just be heaven-sent, as it was for Lucia.

My grandma passed away three years ago now, after battling multiple myeloma. She was like my second mum and I still miss her terribly. In the car on the way to the funeral everyone around me was talking, but I was so devastated I couldn't speak. I was just staring out of the windows, tears streaming down my face. I had never known grief like it. In my head I was thinking, I love you Grandma, why did you have to go and leave us? when suddenly the song 'You Raise Me Up' started playing in my head over and over. It's not a song that specifically meant anything between me and my grandma, but, somehow, the words gave me comfort.

For weeks after the funeral I couldn't stop crying. I was in my car one day, tears in my eyes, having what I called 'a grandma moment'. I put the radio on to try to give me something else to think about, so I could concentrate on driving, and the next song played was 'You Raise Me Up.' Again, it gave me comfort, and made me wonder if perhaps she hadn't left me but was still around watching over me. It may be coincidence, but I like to believe that she is there.

Vesper's account also features music.

Music literally saved my life. I was in my late teens. I decided to go wild swimming with three of my friends. I had done this a few times before and never had any problems but, on this occasion, after I had dived in, I struggle to surface. It felt like something heavy was wrapping around my legs dragging me down. I panicked and struggled as I tried to swim back to the surface but that just made things worse. Then something amazing happened.

The moment I knew I was drowning a peace came over me. I heard this incredible music. I'm sure there were voices singing but not voices that I had ever heard before. As I listened, I stopped struggling and taking in water. I felt hands grabbing my shoulders and I surfaced. My friends had pulled me to safety.

My friends saved my life of that I have no doubt but I feel my guardian angel made their job easier so instead of struggling when they grabbed me, I was easier to pull to the surface. A few years later I heard this beautiful music again when my mother died. I was heartbroken on my way to the funeral but then I heard the music as I was in my car driving there with my wife. It was exactly the same music I heard when I almost drowned. I asked my wife if she heard anything too and she said she couldn't. Was heaven helping me again?

I've also lost count of the number of messages I get from people who tell me that the wise words of a loved one or even a complete stranger can feel like a gift from the other side. And sometimes those words can be ones you simply overhear on the radio or the TV as you go about your daily life. This happened to me once.

After the births of both of my children I would sometimes suffer from severe panic attacks. Despite my research and belief in an afterlife, I feared death and I worried what would happen to them if I died or, worse still, if something happened to them. Sometimes the panic got so bad it would stop me sleeping. One night I woke up with a feeling of inexplicable dread and the worry started again. It was relentless. I got up and switched on the TV, hoping to find some calm. And the first thing I heard were those famous words from the film *The Shawshank Redemption*, 'You can get busy living or you can get busy dying.' It was absolutely the advice I needed to hear. It felt heaven-sent.

In that moment I realised that I had assumed that worrying was doing something positive and that it wasn't and I had to stop. We often think when we worry that it has power, but all it does is prevent us living.

Sage believes she can hear the afterlife in so many ordinary and extraordinary ways. Her beautiful story also shows how everyone can do the work of angels by simply listening.

> *Thank you, Theresa, for reading and listening to my experiences. I've told you everything about my beloved Liam in spirit and how I believe he talks to me through little things, like meaningful songs or sending me comforting voices, thoughts and feelings when I need them the most. I want you to know that it means everything to me to hear him again in this way. It has changed my life.*

CLEAR-HEARING RITUALS

The people in these stories received comfort, guidance, healing and direction from clairaudience. Now it's time to start developing yours. The following clear-hearing rituals are calming ways to hone your hearing. Remember to repeat these rituals for at least three weeks; repetition helps reset your thinking and your behaviour, and tells your angels that you are serious about this!

First thing: The moment you wake up (remember, your brain is in a highly receptive state then) immediately ask your angels to talk to you. You might just hear them call your name, or they might speak to you through inspirational thoughts. Recall and immediately write down any dreams, as the angels may have spoken to you through them.

Music – the food of love: If you haven't seen *The Shawshank Redemption*, there is a wonderful scene where the film's hero locks himself in the prison warden's office and risks severe punishment to gift the inmates a few minutes of opera on the prison loudspeakers. Do track that scene down if you can as it expresses what a priceless gift music is for the soul, how it can take you to your angels immediately. Today, and in coming days, select a piece of music that speaks to your soul and then find somewhere quiet where you can be alone to listen to it. It's no surprise that research[40] shows music can boost mood and promote inner calm because it helps unite the creative and logical parts of the brain. So, let music flow through you every day. Show your angels how ready you are to hear them in the notes of great music.

Dance: Don't fight the urge to dance whenever you hear music you love. Indeed, this ritual is going to encourage you to put your favourite upbeat piece of music on and dance, just for the joy of it. Spirituality is jubilation. Something to celebrate. Your angels don't care whether you have rhythm or not and neither should you. Stop taking yourself so seriously. If you don't want to dance, it suggests you don't want to laugh, love and live your life to the full. So, choose a track that makes you want to move and as you listen to it, even if it is just tapping your feet or fingers, dance along. Here are some daily feel-good, suggestions to get you dancing: 'Hey Ya' by Outkast, 'Don't Stop Believing' by Journey, 'The Bare Necessities' from *The Jungle Book*, 'Good Vibrations' by the Beach Boys, 'Higher Love' by Steve Winwood, 'Simply the

Best' by Tina Turner, 'Dancing Queen' by ABBA, 'Happy' by Pharrell Williams. The dancing possibilities are endless.

Listen: Take a few minutes every day to close your eyes and listen to the sounds going on around you. Perhaps you can hear people talking, music playing, dogs barking or cars driving by. Now take a moment to listen to sounds that are more subtle and easily ignored, like your breathing, the beating of your heart or the click of your computer mouse. In time, start to notice the difference between the sounds of inanimate things, like an alarm going off, and the sounds of things that are alive, like people laughing. Pay more attention to the thoughts, feelings and inspirations that living sounds inspire in you, because these are the sounds of your angels. Let those living sounds fill you up inwardly.

Meditate: Meditation encourages you to enter that state of receptiveness so conducive to hearing your angels and, as an added benefit, research shows it also boosts health and well-being significantly.[41] Contrary to what you may think, it is not a complicated art and does not take years to master. It's very simple and doesn't need to take up hours of your time, either. The listening ritual above was a simple meditation. Here is another one.

Find somewhere where you won't be disturbed and where you can sit comfortably. Close your eyes. Breathe naturally – don't try to force anything or control your breath. Simply notice how you breathe, the movement of your body as you inhale and exhale. If your mind wanders – which it will – return to listening to your breath. Do this for a few minutes and then open your eyes and go back refreshed to your waking life.

Talk less: Extend your enhanced listening skills to the people in your life, too. Instead of thinking of an answer all the time, try to listen more to what people are actually saying to you. Just let them talk and you will be amazed how grateful they will be for being truly heard. Of course, you have to take part in the conversation at some level, but focus more on listening than on talking. The more you practise listening to others in this life, the more you develop empathy, which opens the lines of communication to the next life.

Ask for more: Pick a topic you know nothing about and spend a few minutes each day learning about it. Let this daily ritual inspire you to become more curious about others and yourself. When you meet someone new, ask them about themselves. When you have a thought or a feeling, question it. Make asking questions and learning not an exception but a rule, your new approach to life.

Dawn chorus: Birds and angels have a powerful connection and listening to birdsong is an inspiring way to invite spiritual sounds into your life. Try this at dawn if you are an early riser, or at dusk, because not only is dawn refreshing and dusk relaxing, but these are the times when birds are at their most vocal. But just try to seek out the melody of birdsong whenever you get the chance. Simply listen and drink it all in. If you can't get close to the real thing, listening to audio of birdsong can be just as therapeutic.

Go with the flow: There is a deep, mysterious and powerful world beneath the surface of water, so seek out a stream, river, lake or the sea. Listen and wait to see if the water speaks to you, not through words but through sound, and note the feelings and thoughts that the sound fills you with.

Clear your ears: According to energy medicine, your hearing is governed by two inner ear chakras, which are located slightly above each of your ears. You may want to gently massage those areas every day to release any blockages and clear the sound channel.

Note: If you feel spaced out after performing any of these angel rituals, be sure to drink a glass of water, stretch and yawn. Or go for a brisk walk, have a light snack or do anything that will ground you.

You may notice that when you start increasing your sensitivity to sound, you begin to feel the need to protect your hearing from loud noises or noisy groups of people that perhaps didn't bother you before. Even the sound of a mobile phone ringing loudly may start to grate. You might find yourself increasingly seeking out peace and quiet or quietening down your voice. This is positive, as not only are you protecting your hearing, but you are also tuning into the sounds of spirit from within and all around you, and 'hearing' the voice of spirit with your emotions and your thoughts rather than with your ears.

If you struggle to hear the voices of your angels, chances are you are just not listening intently, or you are not yet ready to hear what they are trying to say. Perhaps you are trying to force things or think it can't happen to you.

Angel voices likely won't come through loud and clear immediately. It takes time to tune into a higher vibration. Keep performing your clear-hearing rituals daily and you will hear them eventually. Every time you do your listening rituals you are making it clear that you want to hear your angels and open up a conversation with them. You also need to release expectations of when or how you are going to hear.

If you don't think you are making progress, notice especially what you say to others. If your words or conversations are not in line with your values or spoken with honesty and heart, it is harder for your angels to communicate anything of meaning to you. They mirror the tone and vibration you set with your words so, every day, make a ritual of noticing whether the words you are speaking are true and ones that your guardian angel would approve of. Also notice whether your words match your actions. If they don't, make a commitment to change your words. Be impeccable with them.

Your self-talk could also be putting up barriers. If it is more negative than positive, make a change; angels are attracted to positivity, love and joy. Fear, guilt and self-deprecation pollute the communication channel between you and the other side. So from now on, every time you hear yourself saying something hurtful or self-deprecating about yourself or others, counter it with something positive to balance things out.

As a rule of thumb, when angels speak the sound is friendly, warm, clear and loving. You won't experience any doubt or fear. The voice may be loud, or it may be like a whisper, but it is always calming. Sometimes the voice you hear may be that of someone authoritative and wise you have never met, or it could sound like the voice of a departed loved one. Sometimes the voice will be very much like your own.

The words of angels often fill you with courage and encourage you to do something – to take positive action. They are also short and to the point. You know you have to do something, even if you aren't sure why. By contrast, when your ego speaks, you experience conflicting impulses and rambling dialogues that stop you doing anything except worrying.

Similarly, if the voice you hear always begins sentences with the word 'I' and sounds angry, negative or harsh, that's your ego doing the talking. And if you don't feel grounded when you hear voices and your thoughts are scattered or contradictory, wishful thinking is taking the lead. Last, but by no means least, if the words you hear – whether from others or from yourself – are excessive, unrealistic, overly flattering and over the top, narcissism is raising its ugly head. Angel words and narcissistic tones are incompatible. They don't understand each other and speak in a totally different language.

WISHFUL THINKING?

People often write to me saying they aren't sure if they've really heard their angels. They ask me if they imagined it or if it's just wishful thinking. My answer is always the same. If the experience brought them a feeling of inner peace that they didn't have before, there is no doubt in my mind the experience was spiritual. If the experience made them question if there is more to this life than meets the eye, it was from above. Angel encounters always make a person feel uplifted, comforted. That is their calling card. Anything that brings anxiety and judgement – particularly if that judgement is self-critical – is not an angelic encounter.

The voices we hear speaking to us can often be confusing and distracting, but you can tell the difference. When angels speak to you, the questions stop swirling around in your head and there is simply a quiet certainty. You just know what you need to say or do, even if you don't understand why you know. This feeling of inner calm and certainty is very different from the noisy clattering of fear. When your angel is speaking to you it is like the words of a kind friend who sees the best in you and seeks to lift you up, not pull you down.

If the inner voices you hear are harsh and use words like 'you are a loser' or 'you suck' or 'you are useless', this is not your angel speaking. It's fear. If your angel feels something isn't right for you, they will tell you that it is time to try a new approach, to find something better. Or there may be no words at all, just a gut feeling that you need to make a change. Your angel is always uplifting, loving and inspirational, and the guidance keeps repeating itself gently and assertively. So, if you aren't sure whether your angel is speaking to you or not, have patience. Give yourself time. If the message persists and remains consistent, chances are it is your angel, because fear doesn't have that inner strength or conviction.

In addition, angels often encourage you to take action, to *do* something even if you are not quite sure why. Fear and anxiety on the other hand keep you trapped in uncertainty and inaction. Angels encourage momentum, fear only creates stasis.

TWO EARS, ONE MOUTH

If you have a question or an area of your life where you want guidance, ask your angels out loud or in your mind. In the days ahead fine-tune your hearing, too. Notice what you hear. Perhaps you will hear a song playing or maybe inspiration will come to you immediately on waking. Or you might overhear something in a dream. The key to clear hearing is turning down the background noise in your life, tuning into the silence and listening clearly and calmly to what is going on around you and within you. It is focusing on what is present, the power and infinite possibilities of *now*.

As you focus on hearing you may find yourself longing for or seeking out more quiet time to reflect. Silence may be as welcome as an old friend, but equally it can be something many of us fear. In conversations it often makes us feel awkward. But it is in the silence, in the pauses, that your angels whisper. Sometimes they have something specific to say but, more often than not, they simply raise their sound vibrations, because they want you to know they are there, listening intently and watching over you.

Speak to your angels every day, with loving and kind words or thoughts and feelings, to help you hear them. Then exhale, trust and listen.

CHAPTER SIX

How to Sense Angels

Sensing is when you feel or know something to be true, but you don't know how you know or why you feel the way you do. It is the most common but also the most ignored channel for angels to communicate, neglected because many of us suppress, fear or simply don't trust our intuition.

Too many of us expect voices and visions, thinking that spiritual inspiration has to be blindingly obvious. We don't trust what we sense or just know, even though those super-senses were likely what kept us alive in ancient times, alerting us and our group to potential danger.

Feeling, touching, tasting, smelling or sensing something that is unseen is called clairsentience. The psychic term used for simply 'knowing' something when you can't explain why is claircognizance. Although clairsentience refers to feelings and claircognizance to thoughts or intuition, the distinction is subtle and blurred because when it comes to sensing the presence of angels, your feelings and thoughts work in harmony. Indeed, you may already have noticed that when discussing channels of communication with the psychic world, there is a great deal of crossover because they are all interconnected.

It's very likely you have already intuitively sensed the presence of angels through your feelings and thoughts but haven't recognised them as such. Indeed, clairsentience is the most common way to connect to angels so the list below is longer than the previous two chapters. Do any of the following resonate?

- You felt strongly that someone or something has physically touched your cheek or stroked your hair; or a tickling sensation like shivers down your spine. You may also get a tight feeling in your stomach or your head or get a bitter taste in your mouth when things don't feel right.
- You could have sworn someone was standing or sitting behind you or staring at you, but when you turned around there was no one there.
- You suddenly feel the presence of a departed loved one around you for no apparent reason.
- You sometimes feel a light breeze but there is no source.
- On occasion, you smell certain scents that have no recognisable origin, for example perfume, flowers, lavender or vanilla.
- Sometimes when you meet someone you feel elated or drained for no apparent reason. The moods of other people, especially those closest to you, influence you greatly. You also sometimes know how another person feels without them having to tell you, and you feel the atmosphere of a room you walk into.
- You may feel unexpected surges of joy and comfort for no

reason – and it feels like drinking a cup of hot chocolate on a winter's day.

- During times of uncertainty you have suddenly felt engulfed by a sense of purpose that gives you the strength to know what to do and move forward. Like a bolt out of the blue, you have an 'aha' moment of sudden realisation, or knowledge, clarity or understanding of what you need to do.
- You know when someone has passed over before anyone even tells you about it. This doesn't happen very often, but when it does it tends to happen in a dream where the departed loved one appears or comes to say goodbye.
- You know what someone is going to say next or what is going to happen next, and you are proved correct. Or when a text comes in or your phone rings you know who it is before reading it or answering your phone.
- You meet someone and have an inner sense that they are lying or can't be trusted, and later you are proved right. In much the same way, you can have a deep knowledge that someone is a positive influence and, again, this turns out to be the case because they have a beneficial impact on your life.
- You have a problem that is causing you anxiety but wake up one morning knowing the solution or best way forward. Sometimes this solution appears to you through the symbolism of a vivid dream.

Take a moment now to reflect on those times in your life when you had clarity – a calm sense or knowing that something was true. Your feelings and your thoughts were harmoniously united. Only angels can work that miracle.

SENSING THE TRUTH

In 1977, Sir Alec Guinness was interviewed by Michael Parkinson. In the interview he tells the story of how he bumped into the young actor James Dean in a restaurant in 1955, about a week before Dean died in a car crash. Dean immediately recognised him and, bursting with excitement, was keen to show him his new Porsche. The car still had a bow tied around it. Guinness explains that as soon as he saw the car he was filled with feelings of dread. He knew that if Dean drove that car, he would be dead within a week. He told Dean as much, but to no avail. The video is on YouTube.[42] It will send shivers down your spine.

And the stories below, while they are from everyday people, not famous actors, are equally mesmerising. We start with Asha, who sensed the presence of her grandmother's spirit.

> *When I was in my early twenties, I used to feel my nana sitting on my bed. It was a gentle feeling. Today, I also sometimes sense her standing beside my bed. This is often accompanied by a slight prickling feeling on the back of my neck, which always goes once I sit up and look. I can't see her, but the sensation or feeling she is there is so strong it's as if she has opened my bedroom door and wandered in to check up on me, just like she used to do when I was a child.*

Amber's experience was a reminder from her beloved brother, while Victor's was of his little son's presence.

> Amber's story: *My brother was a painter and decorator and he always smelt of fresh paint – even when he was not on a*

job. Last week, when I was at home tidying up, I suddenly smelt fresh paint. My children were in the room at the time doing homework and I asked them if they could smell it, but they couldn't. I smelt it again in the evening. I was really thinking about my brother now. I started crying and cried even more when my husband reminded me that it was exactly seven years to the day that my brother had died. How could I have forgotten? For some reason – and this is not like me, as I'm usually on top of things – I had got my days muddled up. In his gentle way my brother had sent a reminder that he was always alive in my heart.

Victor's story: *My son died when he was just three years old. I don't have any spectacular visons to report and I don't hear him talk to me, but I do feel him. He's with me all the time, in everything I say and do. He's my son and my guardian angel. I used to feel lonely a lot of the time, especially after my divorce, but I don't feel that any more now. My son is there. He's for ever alive. Can't explain it rationally and I'm not going to visit a medium or anything like that. I don't need to. I know he's alive somewhere and one day we will be together again.*

Maria sensed her angel from within.

Before I had Ana there had been four miscarriages. I worried constantly. The emotional high of finding out that I was pregnant was followed by the excruciating low of miscarriage, with both the physical and emotional pain to deal with. My body ached to become a mother. It was all I thought about, so when I became pregnant for the fifth time I was, of course, overjoyed, but at the same time the familiar worry and fear began. I'd always miscarried before twenty-one weeks, so a month into my pregnancy I decided to go on bed rest. I lay there day after day absolutely terrified to move. Then, at twelve weeks, the unthinkable happened and I started to bleed. Waves of panic washed over me, as this was all too horribly familiar, but then – and I don't know how or why – I had this deep knowing that panic, worry and fear weren't going to make any difference. If I was going to miscarry I would do so, and panic was futile.

As soon as I made the decision not to waste my energy worrying any more, I had a moment of serene awareness. I knew everything was going to be all right. I was taken to hospital and my deep knowing was proved correct, as the baby was fine. I went to full term and delivered Ana safely.

I didn't have an out-of-body or near-death experience, just a deep knowing that worrying was pointless, and that Ana was going to be fine. I truly believe that deep knowing saved my daughter's life because she needed me to be calm. I was connecting to a very deep part of myself – the part of me that belongs to the angels.

In another incident, now-retired US army sergeant Craig had a feeling and a knowing that might just have saved his life. He was doing computer research alone in a trailer while stationed in Baghdad, Iraq. Although the trailer was air-conditioned, he had a sudden compulsion to drink iced tea in the nearby compound.

He never normally drank iced tea and there was plenty of cold water available. It was 44°C (112°F) outside. He tried to fight the compulsion, but finally gave in and went to have some iced tea. It was so hot outside he had to wait a while in the compound before walking back to his trailer. When he arrived back, his trailer was locked down. He found out that one minute after he had left, a rocket had impacted right next to the trailer and stuck like a dart in the ground. It would have killed him.

CLEAR FEELING

Feeling and knowing something to be true but not knowing how or why is, of course, hard to prove.

I encourage those who are dubious to be objective, study the evidence and then put their doubt to the test. Take some time to work through the rituals in this section of the book and see what happens to you. Do be aware, though, that you need to have an open-minded attitude and a willingness to suspend your disbelief.

Remember that when it comes to sensing your angels, a closed mind – along with fear and negativity – partners you with your ego and not your angels. Here's a quick reminder. Angel experiences are consistent – they don't constantly switch course. They are inspiring and gentle, lifting you up rather than pulling you down. They are likely to appear suddenly out of nowhere, like a gift from above, and feel strangely comforting and familiar, fitting in with your personality and natural abilities, like someone or something you have always known. They improve a situation in a way that doesn't just benefit you but also others involved. You feel quietly confident and encouraged to take action, to do something rather than think about doing something. You just feel, you just know you are on the right path.

CLEAR-SENSING RITUALS

The following rituals can all help you sense your angels more clearly. Try them every day and notice what you begin to feel and know to be true.

Keep a journal: Everything and everyone in our lives inspires thoughts and feelings in us, even if those thoughts and feelings are irrational. Start writing down your thoughts in a journal or an onscreen document every day and if you notice any strong feelings record them, too. Most of us focus only on recording our thoughts, but you need both your thoughts and feelings to work together. As you write, don't judge or try to make sense of what you are writing. The daily ritual of writing what is in your mind and heart simply lets your angels know you are paying attention to both your thoughts and feelings and are open to uniting them. Your journal is also a great way to keep a record of your thoughts and feelings so you can look back in hindsight and see how accurate or helpful they were.

Listen to your gut: You may be surprised to learn that your stomach is a kind of primitive brain with its own intelligence – so the term 'gut instinct' makes sense. If you ever feel sick when you are worried or get butterflies in your stomach when you are excited, you will already know that the area below your ribcage is very sensitive to emotion. Start to think of this area as having a mind and a will of its own. Notice what your gut is telling you. Do you feel happy, sad, angry, nervous or calm when you meet someone new, walk into a room or imagine doing something in the future? Your feelings know what your spirit desires, so listen to them.

Body check: Take a few moments each day to close your eyes and tune into your body. Sense how it feels. Let your body rather than your mind do the talking. Intuitive angel wisdom can speak first through your body, so the more in tune you are with it, the clearer your intuition can speak physically to you. During the day notice any tingles or sweating, or unexplained tightness, or butterflies, in your stomach, or an increased heart rate. Pay attention to any uncomfortable bodily sensations, and also notice what you feel, and where and who you are with and where you are at the time they happen.

Try on new shoes: Empathy is the ability to understand the feelings of others. It is essential for opening up communication with angels. A simple way to fine-tune the skill of empathy is to go somewhere busy and observe someone you don't know – without them noticing you are doing so. Take a good look at them and imagine what they are like and what they do for a living. Put yourself in their shoes.

Mix your senses: If colours had sounds what would they be? If words had a taste what would they taste like? If sounds could be seen what would you see? If smells could be felt what would they feel like? Merging your senses in this way may sound strange but it could be a spiritual catalyst. Synaesthesia is a mysterious condition that occurs when one of your senses triggers sensations, images or experience in another sense. Research[43] suggests that this trait is more common in artists, poets, painters and highly creative people, including sensitives and psychics who see auras, or energy fields surrounding a person.

Step outside: Seek out fresh air and walk in a natural spot every day. Spend downtime in a garden or park or other natural setting. If that isn't possible, simply find a tree to lean against to induce those feelings of inner calm so conducive to attracting angels. Nature is good for us – several studies[44] show that to be true.

Think backwards: This is an intuition-boosting ritual I do every evening. I spend a minute or so trying to remember my day backwards, starting with before going to bed and ending with when I got up. It's not as easy as it sounds. Give it a try. It challenges my logical or rational brain and encourages a mindset more receptive to spirit or what cannot be explained, because in spirit, the past, present and future do not exist. People who have near-death experiences often talk of a 'life review', where they see their lives in reverse.

Touch: To become more aware of invisible sensitivities swirling around you, try this exercise. Rub your palms together for a few moments. Then separate your hands so the palms face each other. Bring your palms as close together as you can without touching. Then separate them again. Notice if you feel sensations of warmth between your palms, and perhaps a sense of invisible bonds, of them being pulled back together. As you go about your life become more aware of the power of your touch and the invisible connections between everyone and everything.

Self-care: This is in part common sense rather than a ritual, but you can ritualise it by thinking of your body as a sacred temple for your spirit. If you eat unhealthily, and don't get enough exercise or sleep, it will impact your mood, energy levels and health in a negative way. Any kind of negativity blocks you from connecting to your angels. It really is very simple: the healthier and fitter you are in body, the easier it is for you to tune into your angels.

Smell the flowers: Flowers and plants in general can help open up your heart – the place where angels live and reach out to you. If you can, surround yourself with living things. In colour therapy green, as well as yellow, blue, purple and pink, are often associated with inner calm and inspiration, so find ways to surround yourself with these colours.

Feed your mind: This isn't so much a ritual as a sacred mindset to cultivate. Think of every person you meet and every situation you are in as an opportunity to learn something new. Look at the world as an open book, a treasure trove of secrets. There are so many amazing things to discover and so many insights to feed your unconscious mind, the storage facility for your intuition.

Feel gratitude: Another sacred mindset to cultivate every day is gratitude. Instead of focusing on what you don't have, every morning when you wake up and every evening before you go to bed let your first thoughts be ones of gratitude for what is good in your life. A recent study[45] proved the effectiveness of writing down three things every day that you are grateful for. The mood of those who took part in the study improved significantly after just two weeks of doing this. Think of giving thanks as a vitamin to feed your heart, the place where your angels live.

Forgive yourself and others: To err is human, to forgive is divine. If others have crossed your path in a negative way you can always choose to forgive them. Don't forget but do forgive because you never know what struggles others are going through. When people hurt you, it says more about them and how they feel about themselves than it says about you. People treat you as they treat themselves. Don't take it personally. Lashing out in anger or trying to exact revenge can only offer temporary relief and does not bring you inner peace because you are investing your energy in others and not in yourself. Let go. Forgive. I've spoken to many people close to passing who regret all the wasted time and energy they expended on not forgiving. And remember, sometimes the most important person to forgive is yourself.

Offer to help: If you have the time and energy (remember self-care comes first), commit to regular volunteer work or make a point of offering to help others to ease their burden whenever there is an opportunity to do so. Notice how you feel when you give others your time and energy wanting nothing in return. That feeling creates an unseen energy within you that acts like an angel magnet because you are being an earth angel.

Unplug: For at least an hour, preferably more, each day avoid your phone or computer. We live in a connected world and technology is awesome but if you seriously want to sense your angels you need to unplug on a regular basis. Being at the mercy of phones, screens and social media drains your creativity. Angels speak to you through your creativity and intuition. Your creativity isn't nourished by a screen.[46] Research[47] has shown that it is nourished by what you think, feel, dream and daydream about during precious downtime away from your screens. To reinforce this spiritual point, I urge you to watch the brilliant documentary, *Unplugged*.

Daydream some more: There is tremendous creative potential in daydreaming so give yourself permission to daydream. Letting your mind simply wander isn't a waste of time, contrary to what you may have been told at school. It can be the best[48] use of your time because it fires your intuition and encourages problem-solving. You can call this contemplation, meditation or simply boredom but whatever you call it, just doing and thinking nothing in particular and letting your thoughts roam can be transformative. We live in an over-connected world and whenever boredom strikes the temptation is to reach for your phone, call a friend, or get busy but this ritual encourages you to resist that temptation to distract and choose quiet reflection time instead. Each day, find a quiet space where you can be alone and set a timer for five or ten minutes. Sit down and breathe deeply. Keeping your eyes open recall a recent dream you have had when you were sleeping. Imagine yourself back in that dream. If no dream comes to mind, enter a scene from your favourite movie and place yourself right in it. If you prefer to daydream about something else go ahead. There are only infinite possibilities. It's your dream boat. Sail away with your thoughts in any direction you want, however surreal, until the timer goes off.

Become present: Most of us devote our energy to regretting the past or worrying about the future, forgetting that the past has gone, the future hasn't manifested and the only thing we really have to work with is the present. So, every day for a few moments make a ritual of grounding yourself in the present. This is the mindfulness you may have heard so much about. It's delightfully simple, as most profound things are. Just become fully aware of your surroundings, what you are feeling, what is happening in your life right here, right now. Listen, notice, sense and appreciate. Your angels can only speak clearly when you are fully tuned into the power of now.

Note: If you feel spaced out after performing any of these angel rituals, be sure to drink a glass of water, stretch and yawn. Or go for a brisk walk, have a light snack or do anything that will ground you.

Fear is a major roadblock to sensing angels. But your emotions and thoughts are not to be feared. And the reason for this is because you get to choose whether to entertain them or not. Too many of us believe that if we feel or think something, this feeling or thought defines us. For example, if you feel angry and think ugly thoughts, you believe you are angry and ugly. If there is anything I hope to impart to you in this book, it is that you are *not* your feelings or your thoughts. You are separate from them. Your feelings and thoughts simply pass or flow through you. They do this for a reason: to teach you something important. Life in spirit is a constant lesson.

Should negative thoughts become overpowering, it can help to open up a dialogue with them. Question any assumptions. Don't believe something because you think it. Remind yourself that if the thoughts you 'hear' or feel are harsh or disempowering and fill you with confusion, fear and anxiety, they are not the voice of your angels. A technique that works for me if my thoughts invade is to give them a cartoon character and a silly voice. It's very hard to take Donald Duck seriously!

If you are concerned that developing your psychic senses is going to attract frightening feelings and thoughts, take a deep breath, close your eyes and observe yourself. Think of your emotions as a stream that you are sitting beside and observing. You choose what feelings you indulge. It's the same for your thoughts. Thinking something does not make it so. Do the exercise of thinking backwards (see page 119) to remind you that you are the manager of your thoughts. Step outside your thoughts. It's all about what you choose to let in and what you choose to let go.

It can feel very odd at first, watching yourself from the inside out, but distancing yourself from your thoughts, feelings and actions gives you remarkable inner clarity. You tune into the silence of *you* – the angelic part of you that glows. When that happens, someone else – typically someone who is also sensitive – notices your inner glow and is inspired by it. There won't be any words or physical interaction, but they will feel connected to you in ways they may not understand. They will sense a spiritual connection that will light them up from the inside out. Then, in turn, they will inspire and light up someone else, and so on. What is happening here is the mystical connection between all people, which near-death accounts express so beautifully – a sense of oneness with everyone and everything that is the message your angels bring.

PROTECT YOUR SENSITIVE SOUL

As you become more sensitive to what is going on around you and pick up on things you have not noticed before, it's important that you protect yourself. The more sensitive you are to what is unseen, the more risk there is of you confusing the feelings of others with your own. For example, if a friend is feeling sad you may end up feeling sad too and not understand why. This is especially the case for sensitive souls who work in the caring professions.

It can help to imagine a protective white bubble around you, especially if you find yourself in a negative situation. This isn't being cold or uncaring. You are not shutting down your empathy. You are protecting yourself from taking on what is not yours. Your angels want you to be kind, but not if you drain yourself in the process. If you feel depleted, you won't be able help anyone, so protecting yourself when you feel fragile is also helping others.

Give yourself plenty of quiet time alone to recharge and find your calm centre as you work on your twenty-one days of angel-attracting rituals, even if that alone time is just a few minutes. Make it a daily ritual. If you have ever read a Jane Austen novel, you will know how often the heroine retires to her room to reflect and write in her journal about events, to avoid overwhelm. Mr Bennet in *Pride and Prejudice* retires to his library after the hustle and bustle of family dinners for the very same reason. Start thinking of yourself and your energy in this same respectful way. Recharge your energy as often as you can.

GO WITHIN

All the rituals in this section of the book have in one way or another encouraged you to raise your vibration, so you can see, hear and feel the angels all around you. But, more importantly, I hope they have also inspired you to look within and connect to your intuition – the still, calm voice that speaks through your heart and knows what is in your best interests. It is 'tuition' from within, your personal guidance system or GPS, the voice of your inner angel speaking to you from the inside out.

Going within is the quickest way to see, hear and feel angels. When you look into your heart you are rediscovering who you truly are – a spiritual being having a human experience. Your heart begins and ends everything, and it is through your heart that angels talk to you. It sounds like a cliché but it is true: your heart answers and opens the door.

TRUST YOURSELF

If you need help or want something to manifest in your life, make a ritual of asking your angels for help. You can ask out loud, in writing or in your heart. Then let go. Don't force anything. Put your request out there. Trust that if it's in your best interests you will be nudged in the right direction, meaningful signs from your angels will come. It is not easy to get this delicate balance between wanting something and letting go. It feels like a paradox. But when you are overly attached to outcomes, this creates stress and tension that repels rather than attracts success. When you are detached you understand that you truly have what you need. You are complete already. Nothing is missing. I hope this chapter and the previous two have helped you trust yourself more so you can sense your angels everywhere. Try not to rush or force things and be patient when you make mistakes – because you will make mistakes and there is nothing wrong with that if you learn from your errors. Think of all the experiences in your life, even negative ones, as opportunities to learn and grow in sprit.

And as far as learning and growing in spirit is concerned, in my opinion nothing can teach you more about yourself and your angels than the subject of the next chapter: your dreams. Activating your night vision is essential. Rituals are things you can do when you are awake, but your connection to angels is 24/7 and doesn't sleep when your body and brain do. Your soul is always wide awake.

CHAPTER SEVEN

While You Are Sleeping

Dreams are a portal, an entry point to the world of the unseen, where angels tread. They are the most common but frequently neglected way to see, hear and sense your angels. One of the reasons they are frequently ignored is because we think our dreams are random. But nothing could be further from the truth. While you are sleeping, messages from your angels can enter your unconscious mind – the place where all true magic begins and where there is no time and space, just infinite possibility. Every night angels remind you in your dreams who you truly are – a spiritual being.

In your dreams you enter a world where the extraordinary is the norm, and cross the boundaries of time, space, life, death. You can walk and talk with your angels.

Let's illustrate with this story from Nia.

My mother's final days were not peaceful. I sat with her as often as I could and for as long as I could stay awake. I'm not sure she always knew it was me holding her hand. It broke my heart.

On the evening she died, after a restless few hours she finally settled into a deep sleep. I remember looking at her face and felt relieved because, for the first time in weeks, she looked peaceful. She appeared younger, too, and the creases on her forehead seemed to fade. I sat back in my chair, still holding her hand, and closed my eyes.

Within moments I was fast asleep. I saw my mother in my dreams. She looked young and old at the same time – ageless. It's hard to describe. I saw her stand in front of me. We weren't in the hospital. We were outside in a field of rich green grass that I can't place as somewhere I know. She didn't say anything, she just looked at me. She held both my hands in hers. We had the most loving eye contact. Then she gently released her hands from mine and turned her back to me and started walking away. I started to walk behind her, but then a loud noise woke me up.

The loud noise was the door opening, and night nurses and medics rushing into my mother's room. This had happened before and my mother had been revived, so I knew that I needed to step back and let them do their work. I took a few paces back and leaned against the wall. My eyes still felt heavy from my nap, so I closed them again. As I did, in the space behind my eyes, I saw my mother again as she had appeared in my dream. This time, just as she had done at the end of my dream, she was walking towards a bright light in the distance. When I opened my eyes again, I was told that my mother had passed. She had died peacefully in her sleep.

Of course, the moment was heavy with sadness, but deep

within me my dream had filled me with feelings of calm and joy.

Reina's dream woke her up.

In 2014 my sister passed away from heart disease. We loved each other deeply and when the two of us were together we could talk for hours. But were both high achievers with busy lives and growing families and there was never enough time for the two of us to catch up properly. We would justify not spending much time together any more by saying one day when we were both retired and our children adults we would sit on the porch and have a good laugh. We never got to sit on the porch together.

I'm messaging you because last month I dreamt of my sister. It was an astonishingly vivid and memorable dream. In the dream she pulled up a chair and sat beside my bed. I was not aware of her death in the dream. It was as if she was still alive. My sister looked calm and happy. She didn't say anything she simply touched my heart with her hand and said, 'take care of this'.

I woke up with her words, her voice still reverberating in my head. For a brief moment I thought she was still alive but then I remembered and felt sad. I got up and had a shower. While I was washing myself, I felt a small and tender to the touch lump on my left breast. Normally I would have dismissed it but the dream of my sister pointing to my heart – my left breast – felt like a warning. It was.

Two days later I was referred for a breast cancer scan. I have now had the cancer removed.

* * *

Do you ever wake up between the hours of 2 a.m. and 5 a.m.? If you do, be sure to write down immediately any images, thoughts or feelings that come to mind. In contemplative orders, regardless of religion, the early hours of the morning when the world is quiet, is the call to prayer. I believe that when you wake early it is important not to get stressed or upset; it just means your dreaming mind has such an important message for you that you need to be woken up. Listen to the images and ideas you have then. They could be transformative and will almost certainly be infinitely creative.

In much the same way, have you ever woken up inexplicably exhausted? As with early-morning waking, any medical or stress-related reasons should be taken into consideration and eliminated first but, if you can't find any logical reason, you may want to consider whether your spirit has had a very active night. This may have been the case for Jade.

I've been a nurse all my life and I retired two years ago. I didn't have time to take care of myself much when I was working because the hours were so long and my job was very stressful. So, since I finished work I've joined a gym, lost weight and started doing yoga and meditation. I've never felt better. I passed my medical with flying colours. I've also started to have some remarkable dreams.

One stands out and it's the reason I am writing to you. Last month I dreamt I was back at work. I was with a patient called Lenny. He was in his mid-sixties and he had Covid-19. In my dream I sat by him and he told me all about himself and his life. He had served in the army and then set up his own business selling stationery. He talked about his children – he had three – and how he was sad he couldn't see them. I told him I would try to find a way for him to do a video call with them. I held his hand in the dream until he fell asleep, as he was in a lot of pain.

About three days later I met a friend from my nursing days. She was going to retire in about six months. I asked her about work and if she would miss it as much as I did. She said she had mixed feelings, but she was happy that she didn't have to watch people die alone any more due to the pandemic visiting restrictions. She then told me about a man called Lenny, who had died without seeing his children only a few days previously. It was heartbreaking as they had not been able to organise a video call in time. I couldn't believe what I was hearing and asked her if this man had been in the army previously. My friend said she believed he had. She said it broke her heart that he had died alone without anyone to hold his hand.

But I don't think he was alone. I think I was with him.

What a wonderful thought: even if you don't recall it, when you are asleep you may have the potential to become an angel and be there for others in their time of need. So, the next time you wake up inexplicably exhausted and have ruled out all medical reasons, perhaps your spirit has been very busy indeed!

And then there are dreams like this one from Gary, which may quite literally have saved his life.

Headlights

I was a travelling salesman a few years ago and I was on the road a lot. One night I had this really vivid dream. I was driving down a road I did not recognise. I passed a tiny church and came to a sharp corner. Before I had a chance to slow down, the headlights of an oncoming car appeared in front of me. The car was travelling very fast and I woke up right at the moment of impact. I was sweating and shaking, as if I had actually been there.

The dream was frightening, but after a few days I forgot all about it, until I found myself driving to collect a delivery down a road I had never been down before. But it was not unfamiliar. I had seen it in my dream. Things got eerie when I saw the church from my dream and, sure enough, there was that sharp bend in the road just after the church. It was just as I had dreamt it. In an instant I found myself slowing down and, just as I did, this other car came hurtling around the corner at a crazy speed. Seconds later a police car followed in hot pursuit. Now that police car had not been in my dream, but everything else had: the road, the little church, the sharp bend and the speeding car coming around it. I do believe my dream warned me to take evasive action just in time to avoid a head-on collision. It was a miracle.

Gary's dream suggests that, when we fall asleep, our spirits can see the bigger picture of our lives and that time as we know it does not exist.

* * *

Whenever I read dream stories, I grow ever more convinced that our consciousness is not limited to our physical bodies. In our dreams we can all cross boundaries of space and time and become our true angelic self – which is a self of infinite possibility. When you are awake there are so many distractions but, when you dream, barriers of disbelief, logic and fear are lifted, offering you unlimited access to the world of spirit.

At this point I'd also like to remind you of what I said right at the start of this book – that your attitude to dreaming may mirror your approach and ability to connect to angels. Dreams happen to all us, whether we are conscious of them and try to decode their subtle messages or not. That's why dreams as angelic calling cards fall into a class all of their own, and why I urge you from now on to pay equally close attention to your night visions as you work through the angel-attracting rituals you learned in Chapters 3 to 5.

DREAM CATCHER

If you ignore the magical world of your dreams, I truly believe you could be dismissing one of the most powerful ways to connect to your angels. Meditation is a fast track to connecting with your angels. The Dalai Lama once said, 'The best meditation is sleep' and what happens when you sleep? You dream.

I've studied dreams for decades now – and written more than my fair share of dream dictionaries – and I'm in no doubt that dreams affect our lives far more than we realise. They can provide extraordinary insights, connections, guidance and healing. Even nightmares are cathartic because, when you wake up, what you feared in your dreams has become a memory, something you have already faced and can understand better and move on from. Dreams help you understand your present as well as your past better too, face your fears, role-play and offer a treasure trove of creativity to draw from. Above all, they help you understand yourself better and isn't self-knowledge the purpose of all counselling and therapy? Sadly, though, as we've touched on, most of us forget our dreams on waking; and this is a great loss. According to the Talmud, 'A dream that is not interpreted is like a letter that is not read.'

Increasingly psychologists and other scientists[49] are regarding dreams not as random brain activity, but as some kind of mood-regulating system or continuation of reality that can help you work through any problems, fears and challenges you may have in waking life. Dreams can also assist in problem-solving, learning, memory storage, changing behaviour and creativity.[50] Have you ever woken up from a dream with renewed resolve? Other research[51] has shown that in over 80 per cent of cases, dreaming of a departed loved one has a beneficial impact on the grieving process. So if there were things you never got to say to someone who has died, dreams offer you an opportunity to talk to them again and keep that relationship alive in spirit.

Dreams are the symbolic language your inner angel uses to communicate with you. They can act like an internal therapist and are far cheaper than a real one! They offer you a mirror and, if you don't like what you dream, making changes in your waking life can affect what your dreams reflect back at you. The more creative and rewarding your daily life, the more enjoyable your dreams will be. This doesn't mean you will always have fun dreams, as your dreaming mind knows that in order to grow you sometimes need to be challenged. But if you are growing in self-awareness and self-love, you can rest assured that you are likely to have exciting dreams. In short, the more vividly you dream, the better you feel about your waking life. I also believe dreams can be a portal to the afterlife, and angels often offer us comfort and guidance through the memories and spirits of departed loved ones.

Think about it. Not only do scientists not know for sure why we sleep (contrary to popular opinion, our bodies and minds don't actually rest while we sleep), but they don't know why we dream either. There is a theory that dreams are meaningless by-products of other brain functions, but if we are deprived of REM (rapid eye movement) sleep, where most dreaming happens, not only does this increase anxiety, but it significantly shortens lifespan. Many scientists now believe that dreaming is as essential for our physical, mental and emotional wellbeing as food and drink. We sleep to dream!

SLEEP ON IT

The advice to 'sleep on it' is age-old. It's also sound advice. When you fall asleep you give yourself the opportunity to consider issues and problems in your waking life from a different perspective – a spiritual perspective. Even if you don't remember your dreams, chances are you will feel better when you wake up the next morning. This is because while you were sleeping your angels spoke to you on an unconscious level, and this can help change your attitude and move you forward in your waking life.

Bear in mind that the great majority of dreams you have are likely to be symbolic rather than literal. I believe symbolic dreams are still angelic wisdom because they offer us tools for greater self-awareness and spiritual transformation. They present precious wisdom by triggering associations and, in so doing, highlight feelings, hopes and fears so that issues in your waking life can be resolved and hidden strengths and creativity discovered.

However, a small percentage of dreams have a very different feel about them. These dreams can't be compared to others because they are so lucid, clear and obvious that taking them literally is the only option. I call such dreams *night visions*, and it is in these visions that angels and spirits of departed loved ones may reveal themselves to you.

NIGHT VISIONS

If you don't know whether you have had a dream or a night vision, or a visitation from an angel or spirit of a departed loved one, the distinguishing characteristic is that night visions are brilliantly vivid and impossible to forget. The dream seems as real as your waking life and you can remember it in detail for days, weeks, months and years afterwards. You don't know how or why, but you know that your night vision was more than just a dream. The meaning is also clear and is impossible to forget or ignore – in contrast to symbolic dreams, which are often confusing, need extensive interpretation and are easily forgotten. A night vision carries with it a heightened sense of clarity and reality that you can somehow feel, touch and sense.

If you dream of a departed loved one your first thought might be that it is an attempt by your dreaming mind to offer comfort. That's an understandable response, but it doesn't explain why everyone doesn't have this kind of dream following a loss. Neither does it explain the stunning similarities of these dreams. In the majority of cases the loved one who has crossed over is seen in a realistic setting, such as the dreamer's bedroom or a natural location. There is also no shifting story or plot to these dreams. The loved one simply appears and either talks or gazes lovingly. This is unusual, as most dreams more closely resemble the random images of a music video. Most remarkable of all, when the dreamer awakes there is absolutely no doubt in their mind that their loved one visited them in their dream.

Night visions are also overwhelmingly comforting. Typically, when a person is grieving the emotions they experience are conflicting, painful and confusing, increasing the likelihood that a reassuring message is angel-sent. So, if you are grieving and dream of a departed loved one, don't dismiss it as just part of the grieving process, or wishful thinking. It is a message of eternal love.

Appearing in your dreams is a gentle way for angels to reach you because when you are asleep your mind and heart are receptive to the world of spirit. Night visions are perhaps the perfect way for spirits of loved ones to comfort and reassure us without causing unhelpful alarm. With the benefit of hindsight, although I thought I wanted a more dramatic afterlife sign, I can see that dreaming of my departed mother was absolutely the best choice for me because I just wasn't ready for anything else.

* * *

FUTURE VISION

Over the years, I have come to the conclusion that not only can night visions make connections between this life and the next, but they can also bridge the gap between past, present and future. Precognitive dreams fascinated me so much that I teamed up with scientific pioneer and leading expert in presentiment (sensing the future when you are awake), Dr Julia Mossbridge. (Dr Mossbridge also co-authored *Transcendent Mind*, published by the Psychological Association, the first book to suggest the possibility that our mind or consciousness can exist separately from our brain and body.)

In the book Dr Mossbridge and I went on to co-author, *The Premonition Code*, we laid out the very real science of precognition and suggested tentatively that if science is proving that you can sense the future while awake, surely this can also happen when you are asleep?

Precognitive dreams – as we saw was the case for Gary earlier in this chapter (see page 132) – are dreams that appear to be set in the future or show you something happening when it is not possible for you yet to know this. For instance, you may dream of meeting someone you have not met before or haven't seen in a while and the next day or the day after, you actually do meet them. It feels like déjà vu because you have glimpsed this scenario before, in your dream.

Your angels are guiding and showing you things through these dream-glimpses of the future.

Many people ask me how you can tell the difference between precognition and a symbolic dream. For example, if you dream of being in a car crash, should this be interpreted symbolically as something in your life heading out of control or on a collision course? Or will you actually be involved in a car crash? As with parting visions, precognitive dreams have certain hallmarks. They are vivid, have a realistic feel and involve stories with a clear beginning, middle and end, whereas symbolic dreams tend to be incoherent or a series of images and feelings. However, you can think of both types of dreams as angels whispering to you in your sleep.

Do be aware that precognitive dreams that are 100 per cent accurate are rare. But this doesn't mean they don't happen. There is data to suggest that they do – for example, many people reported dreaming of planes and towers collapsing just before 9/11 and many people had pandemic-themed dreams involving figures in masks in late 2019, myself included. Far more likely, though, are dreams that offer glimpses of a *potential* future, which will occur if you continue on your current path. These dreams are just as remarkable because they give you an opportunity to experiment with or preview plausible outcomes. I think such potential future dreams can help you make positive changes if the future you glimpse isn't one you feel good about. They show that the future isn't fixed, and you always have the potential to change it through the actions you take in the present – the power of now. Angels always want you to understand and realise the power of now.

DREAM RECALL

As we've seen already, many of our dreams fade instantly when we wake up. But dream recall is something everyone can learn to do. My recommendation is to make dream recall your morning ritual; then it will soon become a natural part of your life. Simply reading this chapter about dreaming may well trigger dream recall for you.

To increase your chances of dream recall, be sure to put a pen and notebook beside your bed. Just before you drift off to sleep, tell yourself that you are going to dream and that it will be fun.

Then, as soon as you wake up the next morning, keep your eyes closed and stay in the position you woke up in. Any movement will distract you and hinder dream recall. Don't force anything, just see what images and feelings come to mind and, when they do, reach for your pen and notebook. Write them down immediately. Don't go to the bathroom, get dressed or plan your coming day first, because your dreams can't compete with practicalities. You have to write them down immediately on waking, otherwise they will just fade from memory.

As you note down what you recall, don't try to understand or interpret it yet. Just get it down on paper. And write in the present tense to keep the dream feeling relevant and alive. Write down any images, symbols, themes, stories, colours, people, places, animals, landscapes and anything else you can remember. Above all, pay attention to your feelings, as they will prove crucial to your interpretation. If it suits you to draw your dream rather than write it down, do that, or use another way of recording it – whatever works best for you. And don't try to ensure that what you write down or draw makes sense. It won't!

Then, when you have noted everything down, get on with your day. Return to your dream journal later, perhaps in the evening before you go to bed.

If you wake up and can't remember anything at all, don't worry. It can take time to reconnect with your dreaming self and for your dreaming self to trust that you are really paying attention. Just write down in your notebook that you can't recall your dream today. Simply writing something in your dream notebook first thing shows your dreaming self that you are serious about recalling and understanding the messages of your dreams.

For the last twenty or so years I have kept a dream journal. I rarely travel without it, and the more I have written down and thought about my dreams, the more I've started to recall them. It is fascinating to look back at my dream life over the years and see how my dream world has complemented and inspired my waking life, sometimes even predicted it. I've also noticed that sometimes it is a series of dreams that offers me the greatest insight and proof there is more to life than meets the eye.

DECODING YOUR DREAMS

As angels speak to you every night through your dreams, I urge you to keep your dream journal every day for at least three weeks – remember, research suggests this is the minimum amount of time for a daily ritual to become second nature. And once you have made writing in your dream journal a daily ritual, the magic really begins and you start understanding your dreams.

This is where many people lose faith, as the great majority of dreams are symbolic and symbolic dreams often don't seem to make any sense. But this doesn't mean that they are worthless. Quite the contrary: once you learn how to decode them, they can offer invaluable inspiration and insight. For instance, if you noticing a recurring colour in your dreams, for example red, the message may be that you need to take action, or inject more passion into your daily life. You simply need to know how to interpret dreams and that starts with understanding that dreams speak in a different language – the language of symbols.

The symbols in your dreams are your feelings and thoughts transformed into images or scenarios from your waking life, which can trigger personal associations. They are like personal codes you need to crack, but the aim is not to confuse you – your dreaming mind is just trying to speak to you, in the only way it knows how.

The more you record and reflect on your dreams, the more likely it is that you will start to recognise what your personal symbols and images mean. Every dream symbol is unique to you. For example, if you love dogs, dreaming of a dog may signify companionship and loyalty but, if you fear dogs, it could be a symbol of anxiety.

As well as understanding that everything you experience in a dream is personal to you, you also need to realise that everything you dream is about you, or a symbolic aspect of you, or something you are experiencing, feeling or thinking. For example, let's say you dream of having an affair with your boss. This doesn't mean you fancy your boss. It simply means that some aspect of your boss's personality needs to be acknowledged or expressed by you. In this way every dream is like a hall of mirrors. You are dreaming *you*. There's a wonderful scene in the movie *Inception* when everyone stops and stares at the dreamer, which illustrates how all the aspects of you are looking at and trying to communicate to you in a dream.

Recurring dreams indicate that there is something important your dreaming mind wants you to know, but you have yet to understand its message. For example, if you repeatedly dream that a loved one has died, this does not mean they are going to die soon, but simply that the relationship between you and your loved one is changing and growing or needs to change and grow. Many parents have this kind of dream when their children go to university for the first time – one stage of life is beginning and, before every new beginning, there has to be an ending.

Have fun decoding your dreams, and remember that the great majority of your dreams are symbolic. Sometimes when your angels speak to you in dreams through frightening or recurring images (the most common include drowning, falling, being late, teeth falling out), they do this not to frighten you but to draw your attention to something in your waking life that needs tending to. And sometimes they send you illuminating images, such as flying, dancing, relaxing on a beach, or discovering a hidden treasure; this is a message of their love.

DARE TO DREAM

You may find that your newly discovered enthusiasm for dreaming triggers episodes of lucidity in your dreams. This is perhaps the most exciting way to dream.

Lucid dreaming means being aware that you are dreaming *when* you are dreaming. 'Waking up' in your dream and taking control of what happens in it is one of the most empowering feelings, and when it has happened to me the confidence boost it has given me and the awareness of the infinite potential within me is a gift from my angels that has filtered through into my waking life.

Season 2 of my *White Shores* podcast launched with an episode about lucid dreaming with Dr Clare Johnson, who is an expert on the subject. You might want to have a listen.

I get a lot of questions about lucid dreaming and how to do it. Like anything, it takes time and practice but, if you follow some simple techniques, you have a good foundation for creating your own virtual reality. You can then experience and safely role-play to be anything or anyone you have ever wanted. You can fly, you can breathe underwater. You can surf the sun, the moon and the stars. You can learn new skills, speak to flowers and find creative solutions to just about anything, because the limitations of waking reality don't exist.

To 'train' yourself for lucid dreaming, try a couple of things.

Choose one or two everyday things such as checking your watch or meeting someone, and make a habit of asking yourself, just before you do them, whether you are awake or dreaming. Over time, asking this question will become so ingrained that you may well start asking yourself the same thing when you are asleep. This helps you to develop your ability to be aware of when you're dreaming.

Another tip is to show your dreaming mind how much you value it by bringing elements of dreams into your waking life. For example, if you have a dream in which you are wearing red, wear red when you get up and dressed the next day. If you have been swimming in your dream, see if there is an opportunity to swim the next day. In this way, your dreaming life and your waking life start to resemble each other, which may trigger episodes of lucidity.

Finally, some experts recommend changing your sleep pattern to encourage lucid dreaming – for example, waking up at 4 a.m. and then going back to sleep at 6 a.m. I wouldn't recommend this technique on days when you are working or driving or operating machinery and so on, but research does indicate that during periods of delayed sleep we tend to have more REM sleep – the stage when dreaming occurs – than we have when we sleep at our normal time. As a result, we are more likely to experience lucid dreaming.

For some people lucid dreaming comes naturally, but don't worry if you try these techniques and can't make it happen. Remember, trying to force things creates tension, and that's an angel blocker. Perhaps you are more suited to seeing angels with your eyes open rather than closed? Experiment and keep doing all your angel-attracting rituals with your eyes both wide open and shut until you find what works for you.

WHAT IF?

I truly hope this chapter has inspired you to pay far more attention to your dreams and helped you think about your dreams in a whole new light. Your angels can communicate to you through the symbols in your dreams and offer you insight, guidance and comfort to help you in your waking life. Perhaps the most exciting part of your day begins when you put your head on the pillow. When you dream you enter another reality where the extraordinary becomes ordinary and nothing is what it seems. You fly with angels.

Let's close this chapter with a quote that encourages you to ask the most powerful question you can ever ask your dreams and your angels: 'What if?' Memorise it and then say it silently to yourself just before you go to sleep. Drift into a blissful sleep, wake up, notice and live your dreams!

> 'What if in your sleep you dreamt and what if in your dream you went to heaven and there plucked a strange and beautiful flower, and what if when you awoke you had the flower in your hand? Ah, what then?'
>
> Samuel Taylor Coleridge

CHAPTER EIGHT

Signs

Hopefully by now you are performing your daily angel-attracting rituals, keeping a dream journal and opening up your psychic potential. This chapter explores another frequently discounted way for angels to speak to us, which is through the secret language of signs.

WHAT IS A SIGN?

It can quite literally be anything that feels like a message delivered just for you, at exactly the right time to bring you comfort and inner strength. The sign may make you feel that a departed loved one is close by or that an angel is guiding and watching over you.

You'll notice that many of the true stories in this book feature signs. It's the secret language that angels speak for a reason. Your angels want you to notice these signs for yourself, because when you do you are seeing the extraordinary in the ordinary, discovering your secret key to happiness.

JUST A COINCIDENCE?

A rainbow appears when you think of a departed loved one. You feel alone and scared and for reasons you can't explain, seeing a white feather brings you comfort. Or in a *Sliding Doors* movie moment you miss a train and thus meet someone who changes your life for ever. Or a song plays that seems to speak directly to you when you need it the most.

Coincidence or an angel calling your name? You decide.

Here's a story to set you thinking, sent to me by Evander.

Every morning I leave my house to pick up groceries and do other chores. I make sure my wife – who suffers from chronic poor health – has had her medication first. Yesterday I gave my wife her medication and asked her what she wanted for lunch as usual. She was sitting on the sofa in our living room and was in a good mood, and that made me feel happy.

I grabbed a mask and put it in my pocket before I left the house. After a few minutes walking I noticed a beautiful white feather on the floor. It was perfect. I stooped down to pick it up, because my wife loves white feathers. She always tells me it is a sign from the angels. I felt a surge of unexpected joy picking it up and was excited to show it to her. I was still holding the feather in my hand when I got to the corner shop. Before entering, I reached into my pocket to put on my mask, but it wasn't there. I thought about buying one in the shop as they had a stand selling cheap ones right by the window.

But something told me to head back home instead and find my own mask.

I opened the door and my mask was lying in the doorway – it must have fallen out of my pocket. I shouted hello to my wife. Hearing nothing, I popped my head around the living room door. I saw her fast asleep on the sofa, which was unusual as she didn't nap in the morning. It didn't take me long to realise she had gone into cardiac arrest. I phoned for an ambulance and did emergency CPR, and when the paramedics arrived they said if I had not responded immediately or come back home when I did, she would likely not have survived. I dread to think what would have happened if I had not decided to go back home for my mask. Imagine if I had gone shopping and come back half an hour or so later.

You could say it was all a coincidence, but I think it was more than that. It was my guardian angel or my love for my wife talking to me in some unseen way. Or it could have been an intervention by that white feather I picked up.

Chaos theory has long argued that everything in our lives is random, but scientists who study it are now beginning to suggest that chaos theory is evolving and there might be patterns to chaos.

It's easy to understand why; just take a look at the miracle design of the human brain or a simple snowflake. It doesn't seem random, does it? It feels like a perfect design.

Every person who has ever sent me a story about a sign or a coincidence has told me things like 'the timing felt perfect' or 'the right place at the right time'. Increasingly, I believe nothing in our lives is random and we are all interconnected by an unseen order and purpose. Yes, coincidence and signs can be explained away logically but, on the flip side, there is no proof that angels can't speak through the perfect timing of signs either. So, until there is, why not consider – just consider – the possibility that it might be something more than that? There might be a deeper or higher meaning behind the coincidence, which Jung called *synchronicity.*

One of the benefits of getting older is hindsight. It's a joy to reflect on your life and see how everything has somehow brought you to the place you are now. Think about all the times in your life when things just fell into place. What other synchronicities are out there right now waiting for you to discover them?

From now on, as you work through your angel rituals and start recalling and decoding your dreams, I'd like you to become aware of any coincidences and 'signs' in your daily life. Start noticing them, approach each moment with reverence and give thanks for the synchronicity. An appreciative attitude is a mover and a shaker in the world of spirit. It invites more everyday miracles.

COMMONLY REPORTED SIGNS

I'm aware that, due to the personal nature of their significance, signs are unlikely to ever become the subject of serious scientific study in the same way as, say, near-death experiences. Signs also tend to be subtle. But despite their subjectivity and gentleness, they can bring tremendous comfort and healing and for that reason alone they are worthy of note. I love collating stories about them. I am also aware that because of their subtlety, they can easily be missed. But rather like not interpreting a dream, missing a sign is like getting a personal message from someone who loves you and knows you better than you know yourself, and not reading it!

START NOTICING YOUR SIGNS

Typically, signs appear during times of grief and crisis, but sometimes they can appear for no particular reason. In these cases they seem to be a reminder that there is more to this life than the material.

Although some signs are very common – and you'll find most of those mentioned below – I can't stress enough that literally anything that fills you with a sense of awe and brings you comfort when you need it the most can be regarded as a sign, as was the case for Samar, who sent me this email:

> *My brother died last year. We were both Star Wars fans and used to go to conventions together. A few days ago I woke up and he was strongly on my mind. I missed him so much and started to cry. In that instant I had the familiar Star Wars storm trooper theme playing. I followed the sound and walked into the hall where I noticed sunlight shining on a musical Star Wars mug my brother gave to me. Although the mug was like a music box that required winding up for the music to play, somehow the light seemed to have triggered the music. This has never happened before. It was incredible.*

Samar asked me if his sign was just a coincidence, so I asked him to tell me how the music made him feel. He said it was as if his brother had heard him thinking about him and wanted him to know he was close by. I told him that it was more than coincidence. It was his angel sign.

Anything that is personally meaningful to you can be a sign. The common factor is that they make us feel better or remind us that we are not alone and those we have loved and lost have not gone away.

The unusual sighting of a white feather, as we've seen, is a much-loved angel sign. Here's one from Melina.

I made a decision that I wanted to change my life and end relationships that were toxic. I separated from my husband and met someone new who is interested in spiritual growth too. It has not always been easy or a garden of roses, but my life is changing for the better. One day while my partner and I were enjoying a break together, we parked the car and went for a walk around the town. On our return we discovered a large, pure white feather stuck on the windscreen, underneath the wipers. It looked like someone had placed it there. I've had a lot of signs like that from spirit and each one brushes my heart and makes me feel that finally I am on the right path.

The unexpected appearance and/or behaviour of a robin is also something I get a lot of messages about, like this one from Susan.

My husband died several years ago. My garden gets a lot of robins, but there was one that was behaving differently to all the others. It flew onto the fence and sat and watched me for a while. Then he flew in front of me, and backwards and forwards a couple of times. Next, he flew a couple of times in a perfect circle in front of me. Then he flew towards me, landed briefly on my chest, and flew off again and sat on the fence. He continued to sit on the fence, singing, for two minutes. I can't explain it, but it felt like a sign from my husband.

And if that story touched your heart, you might want to check out a mesmerising robin video that will make you cry and smile at the same time. Simply type in your search engine the words, 'Grieving mother, red robin.'

In recent years I have noticed an increase in messages sent to me from funeral directors or people attending a funeral about how they have noticed butterflies hovering close to coffins and how this brings great comfort. I also get sent stories about butterflies appearing to people at significant moments in their lives, a sight that speaks to them at a deep level. This is not surprisingly really, when you consider butterflies are a universal symbol of transformation, from earthbound caterpillars into winged creatures that can fly.

Now that you know the power of these signs, I hope you will never think about a white feather, a passing butterfly or anything that makes you wonder in quite the same way. Like Helana in her story below, you will know your guardian angel is walking beside you.

I was talking silently to my angels when a white dove flew up in front of my car. I went for a walk by the river and a beautiful dragonfly kept flying around me and then, while I was walking, a pure white butterfly landed on a bush right in front of my eyes. I am convinced they were signs only for me.

Clouds, rainbows and stars are much loved and reported angel signs that always raise up those who see them. I have personal experience of this.

I wasn't with my mother when she died, for a variety of reasons. In the months and years following her death I berated myself constantly for not being there. The guilt was overwhelming, triggering bouts of sadness following the birth of my daughter. That sadness appeared again on my daughter's first birthday. I remember there was about an hour to go before our guests arrived. I stared at my daughter's birthday cake and thought about my mother's lonely final moments before she died. I hadn't been there to hold her hand. I kept my hands busy by tidying the house, but this didn't keep my mind busy. My grief and hurt became so intense that I found it hard to breathe.

I went outside, hoping that a gust of fresh air would help release the tension inside. Once in the open I noticed that it was a cold but beautiful afternoon with the promise of a warmer evening ahead. The sun was shining brightly in the sky and as I gazed up, I closed my tearful eyes for a moment to escape the glare. The sight that met me when I opened my eyes was breathtaking. There, in the centre of an otherwise clear blue sky, was a cloud in the shape of an angel. It was an astonishing cloud – perfect in every detail, especially the wings, which seemed to spread right from the top of the angel's head to the bottom of its billowing gown. The angel's hands were folded as if in prayer.

What made the cloud even more remarkable was that it was stationary and clear white, whereas the clouds around it were moving. It was also the only cloud shape I could see in the sky.

I'd often read about angels appearing in the guise of clouds, but this was the first time I had seen one for myself. A deep sensation of peace filled me and the burden of my guilt, which had weighed heavily in my heart for all those years, at last lifted.

Seeing signs in the skies and stars fills me with such a newfound sense of wonder every time. It's impossible to watch the sun set, a rainbow glinting or a starry sky without feeling you are part of something magical. It's not just up above, though, that nature can speak to you. If you look at them with angel eyes, trees, plants, flowers, the grass – every aspect of the natural world, even mud or a grain of sand – can offer you astonishing opportunities to marvel and feel closer to your angels.

ANIMALS

One category of angel communication that isn't taken seriously enough is the loving bond between pets and their owners.[52] There is spirit in all living things and I truly believe that not only do animals have souls, but also they can teach us many spiritual, angelic lessons: compassion, tolerance, patience, loyalty, trust and unconditional love. My childhood was blessed by the love of my cat, and later on, when I was going through a personal crisis, the gift of a little puppy called Arnie changed my life. It's often said that if you have not loved and been loved in return by an animal, your soul is incomplete. I could not agree more.

Scientist Rupert Sheldrake pioneered research into the telepathic bond between pets and their owners. There isn't time to cover pets from heaven and all the wonderful stories I have been sent over the years about animals saving, healing and changing lives or appearing in our lives at exactly the right time. I just want to state that I believe pets often step into the empathetic role of guardian angels, loving us unconditionally when we aren't loving ourselves enough. I also believe that the way you treat animals says much about the kind of person you are; if you have ever wondered why posts and videos about animals often go viral, it's because they showcase not just the appeal of the animals but also human nature at its finest and most caring.[53] And being caring is a defining characteristic of earth angels.

APPLIANCES AND TECHNOLOGY

I have collated hundreds of stories about the phenomenon of a clock stopping or inexplicably starting to work again when someone dies. I also have many stories about music boxes playing after years of inaction, as well as doorbells ringing, lights flickering and TVs, computers and phones malfunctioning.

Angels adapt to their times and I have seen in more recent years a remarkable increase in reports of texts and other messages being received that have no rational explanation – the receiver does not know how on earth the messages were sent or who sent them – but in which the impact on the recipient is deeply meaningful. Here is Louise's remarkable story.[54]

I'm a law lecturer. My husband, the love of my life, died last year. I miss him every moment. But recently I have been receiving texts that are overwhelmingly comforting. My son is very technical and even he is at a loss to explain how these texts are being sent. On my daughter's birthday a WhatsApp group was formed for me, him and my daughter. I know I didn't do it and neither did anyone else.

There may well be a rational explanation here, but what I focus on is the perfect timing of the WhatsApp group. For Louise these were texts from heaven. They feel real and meaningful and anything that does that is angel-sent, in my opinion.

ANGEL NUMBERS

Seeing the number 11.11 – when you glance at a clock or watch and it is 11.11, or a text or email is sent at that time – is believed to be an angel sign because the number 11 is the number of divine guidance according to numerologists. Divine guidance is not limited to the number 11 though; I believe that any number with personal significance to you can be a sign. That number could be your birthday, your house number or any number that gives you pause for thought. It is often said that God is the master mathematician, and numerologists believe numbers have energy vibrations that you can tune into.

Numbers of angelic guidance have great significance for Dara in her story, too.

In your book you state, 'Angels may whisper to you to check your watch and notice that it is 11.11, the symbol of divine love and protection.' Out of sheer curiosity I checked my watch – and guess what? Yes, you got it! It was just coming up to eleven minutes to eleven (in the eleventh month, of course). Quite a surprise, but then again, not really. Just thought you may like to know. I will be giving your book to a lifelong friend who has a degenerative illness, and I hope that he will find the same or similar symbols of love and protection.

OBJECTS

Inanimate objects moving or falling, or lost objects surfacing just in time to bring comfort when it is needed most, are also commonly reported. The object can be anything; the important thing is that it has personal meaning.

In Kandy's[55] case the sign was a pack of biscuits.

I want to share this story because it is one that sends shivers down my spine. It's also one that my mother witnessed. Every time I share it, it's like my father is right beside me.

I was in the kitchen making a cup of tea for my mother. We were chatting and sipping our tea and talking about Dad and our love of biscuits. Suddenly – I kid you not – a pack of biscuits on the kitchen surface exploded and all the biscuits fell onto the floor. I have no idea how that happened. Mum and I think it was Dad.

Coins are often mentioned as signs. Marco sent me this story.

My wife passed away five years ago, but I still have moments when I miss her very much. I went for a walk with my two Labradors one day and was thinking about her and felt a lump in my throat. I stopped to let my dogs sniff and noticed a coin at my feet. It looked unusual, so I bent down to pick it up.

It was filthy, so I took it home. It took a bit of cleaning and when I had done it, I saw that it was dated 1984. That was the year I met my wife. It felt like she wanted me to find it.

I have collated many stories about clocks stopping at the exact moment a loved one dies. It does seem like a clock stopping is a reminder that time is an artificial construct that only exists on Earth and that in the afterlife there is no time, no concept of past, present or future – just never-ending love.

BOOKS

Think about the books and posts and everything you read. These found their way into your hands for a reason. I'm sure there are many books which have had a transformative impact on your life and offered you wisdom at just the time you needed it. I'm humbled to say that I have had messages informing me about the way one of my spiritual books has found someone without them seeking it out. A friend gave it to them as a gift or it was left on a train or they found it in a doctor's surgery. And what they read helped them through a tough time. I've even had stories sent to me about my books taking on a secret life of their own. The following is what a reader, Valerie, posted on Amazon as part of a review of one of my titles.

It's Me

Within a few minutes, after asking my recently deceased husband to show me a sign that he was still around me, I had chosen this book at random. I downloaded it to my Kindle.

After turning about five pages in Chapter 1, I found a subheading with just two words, 'It's Me', and they were flashing rapidly on and off. In a state of shock, I kept turning back a page and trying it again, and each time the two words flashed several times before coming to a standstill. About sixteen pages after this, the same thing happened with another subheading, when two words of another subheading flashed rapidly, and when they came to a standstill they read 'Making Contact'.

I am now wondering if any other readers have experienced the same thing. Does anyone have an explanation as to why these words flash on and off when none of the rest of the text on the page does, or has my husband contacted me? The subheadings are still flashing, but more slowly now, even though I have recharged the battery.

I can't take any credit here. The reason why some people experience a sense of connection after reading my book is nothing to do with the book itself and everything to do with their angel eyes opening them up to infinite possibility. Reading other people's stories about meaningful signs gives them the courage to consciously or unconsciously believe in spirit, ask for contact and expect to receive it.

Any book that inspires connection to spirit can be an angel sign, as can a post on your newsfeed that seems to speak to your heart and bring a sense of calm when you are struggling over a problem or thinking about a loved one. The message here is to keep your eyes wide open and see what messages in the world around you – both natural and man-made – speak to your heart. I've had messages about personally meaningful memes, car number plates, and even sweet wrappers, so please don't rule out anything. Stay alert. Angels work in ingenious ways.

EARTH ANGELS

One of the most ingenious angel signs – but one that you may easily fail to notice or recognise – is them communicating to us through other people. There's been a lot of focus in angel literature on so-called mysterious strangers. These stories involve a person arriving at the scene of an accident to administer exactly the right first aid, comfort, help or advice, and then mysteriously vanishing afterwards and also proving impossible to track down or trace. It's as if they arrived out of nowhere, like the angels they are believed to be.

Whether or not mysterious stranger stories have a paranormal explanation is immaterial to me. It's the message they send that matters most – angels reaching out to you through the kindness and compassion of others. Each time someone in your life shows you love, empathy, respect and kindness, whether that be someone you know or a stranger, it is a sign that angels can assume human form. Notice and appreciate it. And let it serve as a reminder that within you is the potential to be an earth angel for someone else in their hour of need. Emery sent me this uplifting story.

A few years ago I was filling up my car at a petrol station. It was Christmas Eve and it was freezing. I went to pay for my petrol and was standing beside a young woman and her young child. As she was paying for her petrol, her child tugged at her sleeve and asked for some hot chocolate. The mother replied quietly and firmly that she couldn't afford it. I noticed both mother and child were wearing very thin clothes and it made me feel sad. But that's life.

I paid my bill and went back to my car and saw the mother climbing into her own car. The child was shivering. I suddenly remembered I had a couple of old coats in my car, so I grabbed them and asked her if she wanted them. I also gave her my food shopping and some cash from my wallet.

The woman was overcome with gratitude. I told her not to worry and wished her a Happy Christmas. As I walked away, I heard her child ask her if I was a Christmas angel. She said I was. I can't describe to you how hearing that made me feel.

In this way you yourself can become a sign, a reminder that angels are real. Perhaps your kind words or actions can help others feel they have been touched by a miracle. We often forget how our own words and actions can truly be the change we want to see. The following mini parable says it all.

A little girl was lying in the street, shivering and alone. As I walked past her, I got angry with the angels. I asked them why they weren't going to do something to help her. The angels replied that they had done something, they had brought me here.

LETTING THE LIGHT IN

Often it is not just one sign but a combination of signs that convinces a person that angels are talking to them. Once you notice one sign – even if it is not so much a clear sign as something that fills you with awe, such as the joy you feel when you witness the beauty of autumn trees or that feeling of pride when you have done the right thing – it is like drawing back the curtains and letting the light in.

You start to see more and more, as Lina did. Here is her story.

Last week I woke up at 2.22 am. I had this vivid memory of a dream and in that dream my dad (who had been in hospital for several months) told me it was his time to cross over. He asked me to make sure I took care of his paintings. I remember smiling in my dream because in the last few years my father loved painting by numbers. He told me to promise him I would look after them. My dad's painting by numbers obsession had surprised us all as he had never shown interest in art before. In the dream his fingers were the colors of the rainbow and I remember my fingers were pink.

The next morning the hospital called me to say Dad had passed away peacefully in his sleep. They think he passed around 3.30 a.m. but I think it was at 2.22 a.m. In the months after his passing I had all his painting by numbers framed. They are truly beautiful. One made me cry. It was a picture of a bridge over a river and the dominant color tone was pink. On the back of the picture my father had dedicated that painting to me, saying that he would love and be with me for ever.

I've had other signs too. I notice white feathers so much more. I sometimes smell his aftershave. On more than one occasion I have felt him hold my hand. And best of all, I am a painting by numbers enthusiast now. I have discovered a love for painting and creating beautiful pictures that I didn't know

I had. When I paint it feels as if my dad is sitting right beside me.

For many people, signs feel like proof of survival. This is something mediums' readings offer, but opening your own angel eyes can help you establish that connection direct.

SPIRITUAL AWAKENING

When you start to get curious about the world around you and notice angel signs, you are awakening spiritually. You begin to see beyond the material and nothing is quite what it seems. You may also catch fleeting glimpses of the interconnection between everyone and everything and to start to see that you are a part of something expansive.

Sometimes this spiritual awakening is triggered by a trauma, such as bereavement, a broken heart or a mid- or any life crisis, but it doesn't have to be.[56] Here's a message Margo sent me.

I recall vividly that when I was fourteen I had what I guess you can describe as a transcendent experience. Nothing prompted it. I just remember walking home from school one day through the local park. It was autumn and the leaves were falling rapidly. One leaf landed on my head. I pulled it out of my hair and marvelled at how enormous the leaf was. During that moment of marvelling at the size of the leaf I felt this ocean of love passing through me. I studied the colours of the leaf. They felt alive. I looked at the tree the leaf had fallen from and could hear it whisper to me. In that instant I felt this overwhelming sense of connection between myself and nature and with everyone and everything. It was bliss. I understood that I was more than my body. I shall never forget it.

I have had other moments of pure peace, connection and understanding but none quite as powerful as this. I remember that day as if it was yesterday. I'm nearly seventy now and can honestly say that during times of crisis in my life, the memory of that solitary unremarkable but miraculous walk through a leafy park has never failed to give me the strength and the hope I need.

BECOMING

There are clear stages in our spiritual journey and they all play an important part in helping us understand who we truly are.

Being: You are focused on your material and bodily needs: food, sex, relationships.

Belonging: You realise that the material aspect of life, as pleasurable as it can be, does not bring a sense of true meaning and fulfilment. You search for that meaning by joining or belonging to a religion or a group, party or organisation. This could be a company or a cause you are devoted to, or it could be a lightworker or guru you subscribe to. In this stage your beliefs, your sense of belonging to something or someone else, define you. You aren't really thinking for yourself yet.

Becoming: You sense that you need an identity separate from the expectations of others and that fulfilment comes from the inside out, not the outside in. I'm guessing a lot of you reading this book are in this stage. It is your spiritual awakening. You want to learn. You want to grow. You want to expand.

Bliss: In this stage, which isn't sustainable in the long term, you glimpse the interconnection between everyone and everything that people who have near-death experiences talk about. It is a peak, a transcendent experience.

Every one of these stages teaches you something important about yourself and should be fully experienced and appreciated.

There is a whole industry around the idea of a spiritual awakening, but at heart it is pure and simple. It's a personal conversation between you and your angels. From the moment you started reading this book, and likely for years before this, you have already been on that path. You just have not realised it or have not been able yet to see your own light. I hope that in that respect this book is like a breath of spiritual fresh air.

THE ANGEL GENE

Dreams, along with signs and the synchronicity surrounding them, are the secret language of your angels, awakening the spiritual sense that is your birthright. Belief in your angels is in your DNA.[57]

A common theme in angelic experiences is belief in something higher or greater than yourself. As we've seen, angelic experiences are increasingly gaining scientific backing; but you personally may have noticed that the sense of something invisible guiding you isn't always experienced 'out there', but generally happens from within. So a wonderful merging of primary, objective truth with subjective truth seems to be occurring. Science is increasingly showing that the potential to be sensitive,[58] empathetic[59]and kind[60] and to believe in something greater than yourself is in our genetic coding; in other words, the language of angels is already part of who we are. These angelic personality traits have survived human evolution for a reason – communities that care for each other tend to thrive. Your task is to reconnect with these angel traits within you and continue to make the world a better place because of the person you have chosen to be.

Perhaps there have been moments when you feel close to comprehending this innate truth, when a glimpse of a heartfelt sign has triggered in you a feeling of deep understanding and inner peace. Remember, many of the people who share their stories in this book did not actually see an angel or a departed loved one. A personal sign was enough to activate the angel gene in their hearts and open their angel eyes.

THE HEART KNOWS FIRST

Your heart truly does know angels first. If you look at the world around you through the lens of your feelings, you will start to notice the signs, the coincidences, the magic all around. These signs may be invisible at first, but they are there. Search for your angels in a shaft of sunlight, the petals of a flower, between the notes of great music, in the stars, in the kindness of others and yourself or anywhere your heart takes you.

And when things don't go as planned, seeing the world with angel eyes can give you the inner strength to cope. Sometimes things happen that are outside your control and there is nothing you can do; but you can choose how you react. There may be a pattern or a reason behind it all. What can you learn? How can this help you grow? Perhaps something better lies ahead for you. Have you ever looked back on a failed relationship or something that didn't work out in your life and thought: *Thank goodness I didn't get who or what I wanted, because if I had, I wouldn't be the person I am today or where I am today*?

During tough times, I often find myself thinking of that undercover spiritual poem 'If' by Rudyard Kipling and those lines: 'triumph and disaster/And treat those imposters just the same.'

Noticing signs, appreciating coincidences and seeing everything that happens *to* you as happening *for* you, as an opportunity to learn and grow, is a spiritual awakening. And please don't forget to pay extra special attention whenever you feel wonder or awe, because this sacred feeling happens whenever an angel is wrapping their wings tightly around you. When that happens, the mists of materialism and fear recede, you understand that there is an unseen eternal part of you separate from your body, mind, thoughts and feelings. You become who you were born to be – an angel in human form.

Now you are starting to see that the angel within you is the angel outside you, the timing is truly perfect to move forward to the final part of this book. It's all about death, life and other everyday miracles.

PART THREE

It's a Miracle

'There are only two ways to live your life. One is as though nothing is a miracle. The other is as though everything is a miracle.'

ALBERT EINSTEIN

CHAPTER NINE

The Afterlife Report

Seeing the world with angel vision – as performing the angel-attracting rituals from the previous section is designed to facilitate – proves that miracles are not the rare and unexplainable phenomena we have been led to believe. They can happen in every moment.

Every day your angels reveal endless opportunities for you to notice miracles until that final miracle of all – your death.

ANGELS OF DEATH

You might not think of death as a miracle. We tend to go through life fearing death, but your angels are constantly showing you that from a spiritual perspective death is just as miraculous an event as birth, and therefore nothing to fear.

To put death on an equal miracle footing with birth is a huge leap. But the miracle of life includes the miracle of death. You are part of nature and in nature you see the dance of life and death in perpetual motion. It is hard to see where one starts and the other ends, as they are intertwined. You can't have life without death, day without night. Whenever your angels send you after-life signs, the purpose of them is always to remind you that you are more than your body, there is more to life than the material.

Understanding that death is a natural part of life and life is a natural part of death can help you get closer to understanding that your consciousness remains unchanged by death. Have you ever wondered which 'you' will go to heaven when you die? The 'you' as a child, or the 'you' as a teenager? The 'you' that existed yesterday? The 'you' that exists today? The yesterday 'you' and the child 'you' have gone, died, but you – your consciousness – go on, and it is your consciousness that lives on in spirit when your body dies. It is your consciousness, the eternal you, that never dies.

Death is a miracle because it reveals the ultimate truth about your life and replaces limiting concepts of time and space with limitless ones of timelessness and infinity. If you have lost a loved one, what I am saying here may resonate more clearly as chances are you already feel their presence in unexplained ways beyond the reach of your five senses. You know that they are alive within you in your thoughts and in your heart and always will be. You know that death ends a life but not a relationship.

Talking about death is always going to bring up intense feelings because death is the great unknown. Many of us fear it even if we believe in an afterlife, but it is just another natural process. Hate, fear, anger and guilt kill life rather than death itself, bringing despair of the heart and an empty soul. In this way there is no death as such, only darkness where there is no light.

From a scientific perspective modern physics suggests that everything – you, me, this book, your mobile – is made up of energy. The universe comprises vibrating strings of energy, and how this energy vibrates defines how it manifests in the world. As your body and your feelings and thoughts are energy too, is it unfeasible to propose that when you die your consciousness or the energy of your feelings can survive in an unseen, non-physical dimension? And is it possible that, sometimes, we can tune in to that eternal energy of the departed? For me, afterlife signs bear witness to the very real possibility that the strength of the loving energy between two people can sometimes make communication between this life and the next possible.

So, if consciousness lives on after death when we take spirit form, how does that fit in with angels? In Chapter Two (see page 45) I mentioned that there is a generally accepted subtle distinction between angels and spirits, in that angels have not lived on Earth and spirits have lived in the human form of our loved ones. But in my opinion angels and spirits are interchangeable. They both represent the infinite power of love watching over us in this life and the next. I also believe that angels work through the spirits of departed loved ones. Many people – correctly – call departed loved ones their angels.

Over the years I have been sent many astonishing true stories about afterlife signs and visions, and all of them point to the very real possibility that our consciousness does go on after death. I've also been sent many near-death experience (NDE) accounts. Uniting these stories is consciousness (spirit, essence, soul, life force) leaving the body and being liberated from earthly concerns, because in the afterlife our spirits concentrate only on love, truth and understanding.

NDEs have some heavyweight science[61] behind them and, in my opinion, come as close as it might be possible for us to get to 'proof' of survival – evidence for the possibility of there being life after death. They are such a huge topic and outside the scope of this book but I wholeheartedly believe that NDE accounts[62] (of which the inspirational story of Anita Moorjani is a fine example – see page 191) can show that every one of us, however undeserving we may feel, is here for a purpose and that purpose is to love. Indeed, the transformational impact of NDEs – where those who have experienced an NDE return with a totally newfound sense of meaning and purpose – is perhaps the best evidence for their reality as hallucinations tend to have the oppositive impact, triggering depression.

And parting visions stand alongside NDEs as gripping proof of life after death because, in many cases, the person does not seem to be hallucinating or in an altered state of consciousness due to medication. Zahara's story, below, is a tranquil example.

My husband, Ken, died of cancer on 26 May 2004. It was his wish to die at home so, with help from the local hospice, he came home a week before he died. We had been married twenty-seven years. There had been tough times, but they were far outweighed by the good and we both knew we were soul-mates. I like to think of that last week as a kind of second honeymoon. He was still lucid, and we talked for hours about everything, including his death and how we would meet in heaven.

On the day he died, Ken said very little. I knew it would not be long before he left me. I sat with him and held his hand. He just lay back and smiled at me. It was a beautiful moment. I did cry, but they were tears of happiness and gratitude for the years we had shared. His breathing started to get heavy and I felt his hand tighten on mine and then he looked at me and said, 'Ma'. I knew then that he was not seeing me any more. He was seeing his mother in spirit. He then looked above my head and it was a look of such otherworldly peace and calmness, I knew also that an angel was ready to take his spirit home. Then, he whispered the word 'flying', closed his eyes and gently died.

It was a beautiful, perfect death for a beautiful, perfect man.

'The angel of death' is a well-known expression and it often has sinister overtones but the visions people report seeing when they pass fall more into the categories of angels of light and peace.

I have a huge file of parting-vision stories[63] that have been sent to me. These accounts are sometimes from people who are close to death themselves, but more often from loved ones or witnesses, in particular the nurses and doctors caring for them.[64] All these stories talk about experiencing angels, whether as sparks of light or an inner light. Without exception the stories suggest that the angels surrounding the dying are ones that radiate love and comfort.

Many experts argue that deathbed visions, like NDEs, are creations of the dying brain – a kind of sedative to ease the dying process – but this does not explain away rare cases, like this one below sent to me by Loraine, when another person also believes they have witnessed something angelic.

I'm a hospice worker and I've watched over the deaths of countless men, women and children. Something happened five years ago, though, which changed my attitude completely to the dying process.

I was looking after this guy who was brought in one evening. He was not thought to be close to death and I asked him if he would like me to contact any relatives. He told me that there was only one person he wanted to see, but I couldn't get him to tell me her contact details. He told me he had not seen this woman for a long time, and I got the feeling that he was talking about a girlfriend or wife who had died many years ago. He wouldn't stop talking about her, though, and it took a while for him to fall asleep.

At about 10 p.m. I heard him talking in his sleep in a very loud voice. He was talking about the mystery woman again. I called for more medical help but by the time they arrived he had slipped into unconsciousness. He was unconscious for several hours and I tried to make him as comfortable as possible. I really wished there was someone I could contact for him, but it seemed there was no one. Then, about three in the morning, he woke up and became very lucid and alert. This isn't uncommon. I have seen it happen many times when the end is close. He looked at me and then to the other side of the room. I swear I saw a figure of a woman bathed in light standing there. I saw the man's face light up like a torch. He was so very happy to see this woman and it was so moving to see his happiness that I started to cry myself.

Moments later I saw his arms raised up as though someone else had lifted them for him. He took one last breath and as he let it out, his outstretched arms came down and folded across his chest. He died with a broad smile on his face. I would not have believed this had I not seen it with my own eyes. I don't think it was a trick of the light. I know I saw someone or something standing there waiting for him, and I believe it was the woman he had been talking about. She came to help him cross over. From that day on I have never looked at dying people in the same way. They can see, hear and feel things we can't.

And this tender story sent to me by a loving grandfather shows that angels truly are with us from cradle beyond the grave.

My grandson lived for a short six weeks. I would have given anything to ease my son and his wife's pain, but the manner of his death brought some comfort. When we were told that his end was close, we all gathered around his cot. He opened his eyes for the first time since he was born and looked at us for several seconds. It was a look of understanding and connection I will never forget. Then he moved his tiny head and looked up at the ceiling. As he did so he started to smile and that smile stayed on his face as he passed away. I know there may be a medical explanation for this fleeing moment of lucidity but what mattered to us all that day was that we believed there was an angel in the room waiting to carry him away and comforting him with a smile.

All the evidence suggests to me that deathbed visions are exactly what they seem to be: a chorus of angels who come to the dying to ease the transition from this life to the next. And most comforting of all, these striking visions are incredibly reassuring to the relatives and can remove the person's fear of dying.

For a dying person deathbed visions can be a source of courage and strength so real that they can even be the catalyst for physical changes. This may be something as simple as a smile, or the person may have a burst of energy or the temporary return of sight, hearing or speech. For me, these blissful moments of lucidity before passing offer a glimpse of the soul's eternity and the splendour that is there in the most aged, tired and diseased of bodies.

WHAT TO EXPECT WHEN YOU DIE

All the afterlife stories I have been sent suggest that on the other side we reunite with departed loved ones and with our angels, and that both loved ones and angels try to send love and guidance to us before we depart the Earth. They also suggest that the afterlife is a place of learning, understanding, growth and joy (one little girl who had an NDE said she saw 'flowers singing') where everything and everyone is interconnected by the power of love.[65] Although these are the consistencies I have detected, it's impossible to be more precise than that, as I am trying to give human words to a place that is beyond human understanding or description. Having said that, there's a 1998 film called *What Dreams May Come*, starring the late Robin Williams, that you may want to check out. I feel that film captures the essence, the colour, the infinite possibility of the other side.

As for the dying process itself, when the heart stops and the brain flatlines, it seems that initially there is no awareness that you have died. You may float over your body or look down on it or on a place or people you love. When realisation occurs that you have crossed over, the physical world starts to fade until everything becomes non-physical. You feel free, yet aware that your consciousness, your mind, is still alive even though it has separated from your brain and body. At this moment of awareness, you feel a sense of light and love – an overwhelming unconditional love that communicates telepathically to you without words. Although a sense of 'I' remains, personality fades and the 'I' that is 'you' moves forward to another level of existence.

What happens in that level of existence differs from person to person, perhaps suggesting that every day of our lives we are creating the kind of afterlife we will experience with our own thoughts, feelings and, most important of all, our actions. Perhaps our afterlife is created in a consciousness that isn't in our brains but somehow exists separately.

Your angels long for you to know that death is not the end, just another phase in your existence

I truly hope all this encourages you to see death, if not as a miracle, then at least in a new light or, in the words of J. K. Rowling, as 'the next great adventure'. Your angels want you to become aware that you are a spiritual being having a human experience, and being aware that in the midst of life we are in death can truly conquer all fear of death.

BUT WHAT ABOUT GHOSTS?

We've all heard tales of hauntings or watched scary ghost films. Ghosts – in traditional thinking – are spirits that aren't fully aware they have passed over, whereas spirits have an awareness of their passing. Hauntings would need yet another book but for now, if you are curious, I am going to reference Dr Cal Cooper, Senior Lecturer in Parapsychology at the University of Northampton, to give you pause for thought. Dr Cooper has spent years researching reports of hauntings and paranormal phenomena and he told me when I interviewed[66] him that, to date, he has found nothing to convince him ghosts exist. By contrast Loyd Auerbach, a legend in the paranormal community, who runs the Office of Paranormal Investigations and gained attention in 1984 due to the popularity of the *Ghostbusters* film franchise, told me when I interviewed[67] him that when he was investigating the scene of reported hauntings, once he eliminated all possible logical causes he could not rule out the possibility that unusual phenomena were occurring.

Auerbach is not alone in his conclusion. There is a whole world of ghost-hunting enthusiasts out there, using cutting-edge technology at sites of reported hauntings. If you've never been on a ghost hunt, you might want to give it a try. As far as I am concerned anything that opens your mind to unseen possibilities is angel-inspired, and that includes ghost-hunting. That's as long as you approach it in a light-hearted, curious way and remember that when it comes to understanding the afterlife, love and fear cannot coexist.

GRIEVING WITH SPIRIT

It's a wonderful development that increasing numbers of people are prepared to talk openly about their belief in angels and life after death. The more we open our minds to life in spirit, the more experiences will occur. Indeed, just reading this book will let your angels know that your understanding of life and death is changing and growing, and that you may be ready for contact, or to receive signs of 'life' from the other side, yourself. The key word here, though, is 'ready'. Angels only reveal themselves through the spirits of departed loved ones when it is your time to sense them in this way.

When a loved one dies the pain and sense of loss can be gut-wrenching. You may find yourself experiencing emotions you never thought you'd feel. There is much talk of the five stages of grief – denial, anger, bargaining, sadness and acceptance – and while we all navigate these, there is no clear-cut path for anyone. Grief can express itself in thousands of different ways. Everyone's experience of loss is deeply individual, and the 'time heals' advice doesn't necessarily help either. You don't ever really get over the loss of a loved one; you learn to live with it. The loss becomes a part of who you are and one day you can get to a beautiful place – perhaps the sixth stage of grief – where you can think of them with joy before sadness.

Hopefully the information here will help you get to that place of inner peace by showing you how your angels can keep departed loved ones alive in your heart and remind you that your relationship with them does not have to end with their death. You can experience them in a different form, enter into a new relationship with them in spirit.

Many people write to me asking why they can't sense or feel their departed loved one around them, or when they should expect signs from them. My answer is always the same. Spirits of departed loved ones can communicate with us immediately after they pass – there are no limits to time in the world of spirit and they are as eager to reach us as we are to reach them. The issue, then, is not with the spirits but with *us*.

Before spirits can make contact with us, there needs to be a period of acceptance and understanding of their passing. Your relationship with their physical form has ended and you need to accept that. It is truly wonderful when a departed loved one sends us a sign but, as amazing as this contact is, it cannot ever bring them back. Once you come to terms with the physical loss, and feel strong enough emotionally, spirits of departed loved ones are more likely to appear, and your dreams are typically the first gentle point of contact. They can't break through if there is no acceptance of the loss, if grieving is not allowed to happen. They are waiting for the right conditions, for you to be in the right frame of mind.

So how can you achieve this frame of mind?

The first and only step is to experience the grief. You need to cry. You need to mourn. Grieving is like the pain of labour before the joy of holding a new baby in your arms. You need to learn to accept grief and loss as a necessary spiritual awakening or a turning point in your life.

There are no rights or wrongs when it comes to moving through the various stages of grief, but you must give yourself all the time and self-care that you need. Grieving can't be hurried. You can't just snap out of it or get over it. You need to take things one moment, one minute, one hour and one day at a time. There are no quick-fix cures to deaden or escape the pain. An old Turkish proverb states: 'He who conceals his grief finds no remedy for it' and like many proverbs, this is so true. Denying your emotions does not destroy them. If you don't let out your feelings, they could come out at some other time or in another way.

Remember, as long as your actions are not harmful to yourself or others, it is okay to feel angry. It is okay to cry. It is okay to scream out loud. You are not losing control – you are reacting to your loss. Tears are healing.

If you experience a sense of guilt or worthlessness because you are alive and your loved one is not, remember it was your loved one's time to pass and not yours, and nothing you could have said or done would have prevented it. You are unique. There is not and never will be again another person like you on this wonderful Earth, and the world of spirit wants your energy and your spirit to remain here for the time being. There is still a purpose and a destiny for you to fulfil and other people need to see the angel in you. You may feel alone but perhaps one day you can help someone else move through and beyond their grief.

Working through grief cannot be achieved without pain and hurt and it takes time, sometimes a long time. But trust me, I've lost people I thought I couldn't live without and the pain does ease and there is life beyond death; but it will be a new life for you and a new life for your loved one in spirit. Trying to get back to 'normal' or 'your old self again' or the way things used to be after your loved one has passed isn't a goal you should aim for because it is an impossible one. Your life has changed for ever.

You are changed by the loss. The choice for you now is whether this change is going to be a positive or a negative one.

You can choose to celebrate the time you shared with your loved one on Earth or you can choose to live in sadness and bitterness. It's obvious which approach your angels would prefer you to take. What better memorial to their life than you remembering them with feelings of joy? Remember, moving through your grief does not mean that you go into denial, or try to forget the person who has died, it simply means being able to remember them without feelings of intense pain. It is also a deep knowing that each time you remember them, see them with your inner eye, dream about them, sense them or are motivated by feelings of unconditional love, kindness and integrity towards yourself and others, they are alive within and around you.

Again, I want to stress that this takes time. You can't and shouldn't try to hurry the process. Grief is much like the ebb and flow of the sea – sometimes the waves lap gently on the shore, but sometimes they crash hard. With time you will come to a place where memories of your loved one are gentle and sweet. You will also come to a place where you reclaim a part of yourself.

When you love someone deeply, you give away a part of yourself. This 'giving over' of yourself is one of the most beautiful things about love as long as you don't take it to extremes. If too much of your self-worth and happiness are bound to someone else, it isn't healthy for them or you because you are confusing love with need. True love, and the most powerful and healing love of all, is the love that can set a spirit free. When a loved one dies, amid all the pain your loved one gives you an opportunity to reclaim the part of yourself you gave to them, the creativity and the passion that is yours. Clearly this takes time, but if you allow yourself to work through your grief, you will eventually find that your inner strength and potential return to you. You will rediscover who you really are in spirit and there can be nothing more comforting than that.

And finally, I just want to mention the many stories I receive from grieving people who say they would give anything to spend a few more moments with their departed loved one. Afterlife signs give them comfort and hope that one day they may meet again. The most heartbreaking accounts come from people who had absolutely no idea their loved one was going to die because they passed in sudden, unexpected ways. These stories are yet another reminder that every moment you spend with loved ones is an everyday miracle. You never know with absolute certainty if it will be your last. Treasure each moment with them and indeed every moment you are alive on this beautiful Earth.

The present truly is angel-sent – the most miraculous gift.

SHOULD I VISIT A MEDIUM?

A medium is someone who claims that they can see, hear or sense angels and the afterlife. The jury is still out for me as far as mediums are concerned. I don't typically recommend visiting one, especially in the first year of your loss, as your emotions are too raw and you are too vulnerable. Also, your departed loved ones need time to transition to their new life and spirit. It's a shock for them as well. I believe the most powerful way to connect to the afterlife is direct, through your own personal experience, dreams and signs. However, I know that some people find visiting a medium healing.

There are honest mediums out there, but overall I still find myself returning to my default position of endorsing direct contact with the afterlife rather than visiting a medium.

A recent IONS study strengthened my resolve. From 2018 to 2020 Dr Arnaud Delorme[68] completed data collection on twelve mediums and twelve controls.[69] Participants were asked to discern the cause of death of a deceased person by looking at a photo of them taken when they were alive. Fascinatingly, the non-medium, control group performed better than the mediums. It seems the mediums were nervous under laboratory conditions, because when the study was repeated in the comfort of their own homes, they did better. The team concluded that this showed that humans have latent mediumistic skills and the reason the control group did better in the lab was because they did not have performance anxiety to block them as the mediums did. I love this study as it shows how straining too hard or being required to 'perform' can create blocks; but, more than that, it shows that we all have mediumistic potential.

However, if your heart is set on consulting a medium, I strongly urge you to follow the guidelines I suggest on page 229, which don't just apply to mediums but to psychics and all lightworkers.

Regulation

Wouldn't it be amazing if there could be a way to prove mediumistic ability was real? The late sceptic James Randi tried to set this up with his million-dollar challenge for proof of psychic ability, but although many came forward no one won. This is often held up by sceptics as proof that psychic abilities are not genuine, but I think the world of science is the place to look for proof, and Randi was not a scientist but a magician.

I am keen to promote objective scientific research into channelling, psychic abilities and mediumship. My hope is that one day therapists and doctors could share this kind of research about the possibility of an afterlife to ease the grieving process. Wouldn't it be wonderful if there were scientifically validated mediums, as Dr Julie Beischel[70] from the Windbridge Research Center is currently working towards, or precogs, as I tried to initiate during my collaboration with Dr Julia Mossbridge.[71]

Following or having readings with any medium or lightworker may be the right path for you, but *please* do your homework first, remember that at this point you are potentially vulnerable, and be alert about becoming dependent. Especially avoid healers who tell you that you are in need of their healing and they are the only ones that can heal you. And if they bombard you with advertising or ask for your credit card details, I recommend you cut contact with them.

Remember your angels don't want you to follow anyone. Their aim is always to help you follow your own better angels, see the divine wonder within and around *you*.

Life is about evolution. Your angels want you to light up your own way, talk to them directly. They want you to find ways to love and heal yourself, to seek out your own truth.

And that sublime voyage of self-discovery is what the next chapter celebrates.

CHAPTER TEN

Attracting Miracles

Science in its purest sense is the ultimate search for truth. Surely that search for truth should include all experiences, even those that can't be seen, don't seem rational and can't be recorded in a laboratory? I hope what you've read so far has made you aware of the huge amount of evidence that there is something unseen at work in our lives, which goes beyond the material. All the indications are that our consciousness might just be capable of existing independently of our bodies and of linking us to something greater than ourselves, something infinite.

When unseen things happen to you that give you pause for thought or make you wonder if this life is all that it seems, you have a clear choice. You can ignore them or explain them away, or you can choose to interpret them as meaningful. Much that happens to us in life is outside our control. The only thing we truly have control over is how we react. So given that life is unpredictable, why not believe in wonder? Why not believe in angels and everyday miracles?

If you open your mind and heart to them, angels can fly into all areas of your life, bringing their magic with them. Here are some ways you can invite them.

ANGELIC ATTRACTION

Many people have told me they believe angels have played a part in their relationships, helping them find partners, friends and colleagues through wonderful coincidences and signs.

Perhaps you have noticed this yourself? How much have accidents of time and place played a part in your relationships? There are billions of people on the planet and yet somehow you met someone who is perfect for you. It feels miraculous – and it is. However, I am extremely cautious about using terms such as 'soulmate' or 'twin flames'. It's beautiful when two people find each other, but the idea that someone 'completes' you is potentially toxic, as the only person who can complete you is yourself. In addition, relationships are a constant work in progress. They aren't always sunshine and roses and they only work when two people give each other enough space to change and grow together.

Having said this, loving relationships are a mighty source of happiness, so asking your angels to help you with matters of the heart, perhaps by ensuring you are in the right place at the right time to meet someone, is highly recommended. One technique I recommend is to be specific about what you want your angels to send you in terms of a partner. Give your angels clear guidelines. Write down or visualise the qualities you are seeking in a future partner. Then, in your daily life, don't settle for anything less than the best.

If you ask your angels to help you in the love department, the place they will get to work is with the relationship you have with yourself. Contrary to what you may have been led to believe, other people don't treat you as you treat them, they treat you as you treat yourself. You can be the most giving, loving and kind person in a relationship, but until you can also give love and kindness to yourself, the relationship will flounder.

If you ask for your angels' help with affairs of the heart, their message will be simple. They will likely encourage you to take the focus away from finding someone and shine the light on yourself instead. They will find ways to remind you that if you want happiness in love, you need to fall in love with yourself first.

Practise self-care. Become the best you can be. Do things that make your heart sing. As far as others are concerned, don't take things personally (what others say and do is always far more about them than about you). Let go of any expectations of how you think they should behave or treat you, because you have no control over how others should behave. The single biggest relationship mistake is thinking you can change someone, or in other words falling in love with who they could be and not with who they are. The only person you can change is yourself. Fall in love with yourself and your own potential first. Do that and your angels will ensure that love will find you.

Self-love is not about 'shoulds' and 'oughts'. It is simply treating yourself with respect, valuing yourself; becoming your own best friend, your own guardian angel. It's not to be confused with narcissism,[72] as narcissists have zero empathy and a complicated relationship with the truth. Angels can't reach them, and neither should you. Steer clear.

You may find that the love of your angels expressed through placing your focus on self-love is enough to sustain you, or you may find your self-love attracts like-minded souls. Neither life choice is better or worse as far as your angels are concerned. All they are interested in is whether the choices you make with your relationships are ones that help you learn and bring you inner peace.

And if you have had your heart broken, remember your heart is a muscle. The more you use it, the stronger it grows. Your angel will always encourage you to take your broken heart and turn it into art, transform it into something wiser and greater than before. And when you encounter challenges in your relationships or have to deal with difficult people one angelic technique I highly recommend to help you cope is to see the inner child in everyone you encounter. The inner child is where angels connect to you and everyone else. It is the part of you and other people that is vulnerable and which is simply yearning for compassion and love. So often when people behave irrationally they are crying out for attention or simply feeling alone and scared. When you see everyone, including yourself in this understanding light everything becomes so much calmer and clearer.

ANGEL HEALING

Many nurses, doctors and caring professionals have messaged me with incredible true angel-healing stories.[73] In 2015 I interviewed Anita Moorjani,[74] who had had a near-death experience. She told me that before her NDE she was riddled with cancer, but afterwards it just vanished. Her doctors were speechless.

What makes her case so compelling is she has the medical records to prove it!

I'm not going to suggest here that when you get ill or want to lose weight or feel better you can simply pray to your angels and be instantly cured or transformed. As previously mentioned (see page 47), for reasons we may never understand in this life, angels sometimes intervene and sometimes they don't. However, alongside medical intervention and doing all you can yourself to take care of and protect your health – for example, eating healthily, exercising regularly, staying away from toxic substances and getting a good night's sleep – praying to angels for help can make any suffering easier to bear. Spiritual healing is the greatest gift from your angels. There have been studies on the power of prayer to influence physical health and the results so far are inconclusive. But some research[75] also seems to suggest that patients who are prayed for recover faster. So, there is nothing to lose and everything to gain by praying to your angels to improve your health and the health of your loved ones.

And if a loved one is suffering, and you feel helpless and wish you could do something to ease it, there is something you can do. You can ask your angels to help them. You can pray for them.

ANGELS AT WORK

If you are unhappy in your professional life, talk to your angels. You don't need to speak to them out loud, pray on bended knee, light candles or even meditate. You just need to communicate with them silently through your thoughts and feelings.

Before you talk to them, you may wish to write down your career goals or thoughts. It's much easier for your angels to help you if you are specific about exactly *how* you want them to help. Writing or typing your goals is much more powerful than you may think. It helps you organise your thoughts and commit to them. Indeed, writing down your goals or a to-do list each night for the following day is a proven way to become more successful.

One way your angels may help you when it comes to your career is to ignite your curiosity, so you are better placed to notice signs from them. For example, you may notice a training course that interests you, or meet someone who offers you advice, or overhear a conversation online or on the radio that pulls you in the direction of the place you need to go. When I left university, I remember missing a train and feeling angry that I had to wait for the next one. But I am so glad I did, because while I waited I sat on a bench and overheard a conversation between two students discussing a job opportunity at a publishing house that required knowledge of what they described as 'New Age mumbo-jumbo'. This was in the pre-online era and there is no way I would have found out about that opening if I hadn't missed that train.

It's possible that nothing that happens to us, even something as apparently trivial as missing a train, is an accident. Of course it can't be proven, but what if it is true? And if it is, valuing every moment, however seemingly unimportant or trivial, is a fulfilling and happy way to live because it could potentially be life-changing. The more we are able to focus our full attention on the deep meaning and potential of the present, the greater our chances of creating a wonderful future for ourselves.

Another thing that your angels can do to help you with your career is to encourage you to be true to yourself. If you are waking up each morning before work with a sense of dread because you hate your job, keep asking them to help you make a change. The key word here is 'you'. Remember, your angels won't take away your free will and do everything for you, but they can help fill you with a sense of purpose and passion. So often when people make the wrong career choices or feel stuck as far as their career is concerned, it is because they feel they aren't in control of their lives. The angels can help you see that you *are* in control. You can make decisions for yourself. Sometimes making changes can be tough, and you need discipline and patience to follow them through, but the important thing is that you never forget you are in the driving seat.

If you aren't sure what work you should be doing, experiment until you find something you love. The old concept of one career for life is fast disappearing and many of us will retrain and switch several times. Change is positive because every life path you choose is an opportunity for learning and growing. And as fulfilling and important as your career is, ultimately your angels pay more attention to your self-development than to the work you do. It's such a cliché but nevertheless profoundly true – and hospice workers and doctors[76] would agree – that nobody on their deathbed says, 'I wish I had spent more time at the office.'

MONEY, MONEY, MONEY!

Angels can sometimes guide you to unexpected gifts and sources of money, but if you believe that more money, status and popularity is the answer to your prayers, reflect on all the stories in the media about spectacularly rich, successful, beautiful, loved celebrities, who still struggle with depression or addiction and, in some sad cases, take their own lives. You can never know the pain someone else is going through. That's why the spiritual rule of thumb is to always treat others with kindness as you simply don't know what hidden pain may lie beneath the words and actions of others.

Money, status, talent, good looks and popularity are not going to make you happy. That's why your angels aren't likely to help you get rich quick or become super-popular. They want you to focus instead on the things in your life that are priceless. We all have those. For me it is my family and my pets. I love my work, but I can honestly say if I had to choose between that elusive number-one *New York Times* bestseller slot and my little dog, Arnie, I would always choose my Arnie. Knowing this means I am already wealthy.

In the spirit world money has no value or significance whatsoever. That's why praying to angels to help you win the lottery or receive a windfall typically doesn't work. They aren't interested in money. They are only interested in you, and if financial concern is causing you stress, they will help by giving you the motivation to make the important decision you need to so you can live within your means. They may also inspire you to seek new sources of income, get access to financial advice or to organise your finances better, and so on.

It is the wealth of your soul, not your bank balance or your Instagram followers, that interest angels. In the afterlife the only currency is love.

AN ANGEL TO WATCH OVER YOU

The traditional role of your guardian angel is one of protection and safe keeping. It is so comforting to know that you are never alone. Our celestial guides can't always keep us safe from danger, but from the many 'angel-saved-my-life' stories I've been sent over the years, it is clear to me that sometimes they can and do.

Why angels save and protect lives on some occasions and not on others is a mystery that we simply cannot understand in this life, but when I look at the stories I've received and compare them with my own experiences, what I have discovered is that generally it is a clear and loud inner voice that is the decisive factor. There is a moment when the person involved has the choice of following that inner voice or ignoring it. The lesson to be learned from this is that if you do hear a strong inner voice telling you to do something or take action, you may want to listen to it. It's your angel talking to you.

Angels can protect us from physical danger, but their chief concern is to bring hope, love and comfort when we feel alone or are in emotional distress. Nowhere have I found this to be truer than in stories sent to me by people grieving the loss of a loved one. So often they tell me that in the midst of their grief they asked their angels for help and suddenly and unexpectedly felt an invisible warmth or presence that they could not explain, which gave them tremendous comfort. It could be an invisible hand on the shoulder, an unseen kiss or the simple feeling that they are being given a warm and loving hug. In many cases, when these incidents occur, the person had switched off their mind in some way. Perhaps they were drifting off to sleep, standing in a queue or doing routine chores. It seems the angels find it easier to reach out and take away our fears when we let our minds relax.

EVERYDAY MIRACLES

Your angels can help you with every aspect of your life, not just the major ones. And yes, that includes things you might consider trivial, such as finding lost objects, locating a parking space or deciding whether or not to call someone. Your celestial guardians are there to help you whenever you call on them and they can assist you lovingly with whatever makes you feel happy and protected. There are angels for everyone and for everything, so never hesitate to open your heart and ask for their assistance. Whether your request is life-changing or relatively trivial, they are always listening.

And the more in tune you become with the idea that there are angels within and all around you, the more intently they will listen to you and the more clearly you will hear them. If this book has inspired you to look within and all around you for the presence of angels, then your spiritual journey is in progress. In the days, weeks, months and years that follow, you will find ever-increasing ways to attract miracles into your life. Your inner angel will speak to you loud and clear through your intuition and your angel eyes will notice people, things, books, events and ideas that can guide, heal and inspire you.

INNER SMILE

How will you know when you are starting this spiritual journey in earnest? The answer is simple: you will find more and more reasons to smile. As your heart opens up to your angels, laughter and feelings of joy will re-enter your life.

Search for a picture of the Mona Lisa, one of the most famous portraits of all time. I was never previously sure but now I understand the Mona Lisa's smile. It's not a beaming smile, it's an inner smile. There is only a hint of it on her lips, but it is mesmerising. I wouldn't be surprised if she was thinking about angels when the portrait was painted.

Do you know that G. K. Chesterton quote, 'Angels can fly because they can take themselves lightly'? Many people think angels are very serious, but there is reason to believe that they do take themselves lightly. We don't have difficulty thinking of them as loving, comforting and reassuring us, so wouldn't it follow that they also have a sense of humour? Seriousness of purpose and humour can and do go together.

I've been sent many amusing stories about angels. One common occurrence is for phones to ring at inappropriate times and defuse overly serious situations. I had one lovely story sent to me about a funeral where sadness was the order of the day – that is until the middle of the service, when a mobile went off, despite the vicar having asked everyone to switch off their phones. The ringtone was 'Crazy Frog'. Everybody frantically checked their phones were switched off and the culprit turned out to be the vicar himself, who apologised, red-faced. But it didn't matter because by then everybody had collapsed with laughter, which according to his partner was just what the person being buried would have wanted. She had often told him that she didn't want a solemn funeral.

We are all guilty of taking ourselves way too seriously at times, but angels are never closer to you than when you can laugh at yourself or when you are having honest fun. Isn't it those times when laughter has been the order of the day that are most memorable? Humour is a vital ingredient for spiritual and personal growth, although one that is all too often neglected.

As long as the humour is good-natured, I thoroughly recommend listening to a comedian rather than a guru. I don't think many comedians realise it, but they are doing the work of angels.[77]

CHILDREN

It's natural to talk about children so soon after mentioning the importance of laughter in your angel work. Like angels, children love to laugh. It is believed they laugh up to 400 times a day, compared to the adult average of fifteen.

Young children have the innocence, trust, spontaneity and ability to suspend disbelief and see miracles in everyone and everything that we so often lose as we become adults. We replace all this angel potential with doubt and fear. If a child does present you with something that does not conform to logic or reason, try not to tell them it is nonsense or shut down their wonder. I love hearing children talk about angels. They mention them in such a matter-of-fact way, without any doubt that what they are experiencing is real, as this story from Naomi illustrates.

One Saturday, I was driving my six-year-old daughter Chloe to her swimming class. We were talking about birds. I'm an avid birdwatcher and she asked me why I enjoyed it so much. I told her that birds were beautiful creatures with wings and watching them made me feel peaceful and happy.

'You mean like seeing angels,' she said.

I wasn't sure what to say but, before I could reply, she told me in a very matter-of-fact way that she could see angels. I'd never spoken to her about angels before and neither had my wife. We weren't into that kind of stuff. I asked her when she could see angels and she told me it was just before she went to sleep. Her angel would sit on the bed with her.

Many parents write to me about their children seeing angels and ask if I think they are making it all up. I tell them that the best way to determine if these are true angel experiences is the child's response. Is the child unsettled in any way? If there is fear or panic, then the experience is not typically angel-based and may be more to do with attention-seeking or too much exposure to frightening images on screen. But if the child is matter-of-fact and feels safe and comforted or even entertained by the experience, then I believe the experience to be genuine.

I'd encourage all parents to let their children talk to their angels, their imaginary friends. Many parents react with suspicion whenever a child opens up and talks about what they can see and sense from the world of spirit, and this distrust can cause anxiety and confusion for the child. They start to doubt themselves, and the more they doubt themselves and their ability to see magic all around them, the less they are able to see.

The more children are encouraged to stay young at heart, the easier it is for them to stay in touch with their inner child as they grow up. It is through your inner child that your angels speak to you and encourage you to notice them. So, even if you can't see what the child is seeing, if they tell you about seeing or hearing angels, encourage them to talk about their experiences. Help them stay receptive to the world of magic, wonder and possibility. Children today urgently need to stay open to the message of love and goodness that angels bring. All children need to understand that even though angels can't solve the world's problems, trusting in them can give them inner strength.

And if in you come across terms such as 'indigo', 'crystal-star' or any other special term used to describe children born in a certain decade or span of years, who are allegedly born with superior paranormal powers or gifts, move on swiftly. Every child, regardless of when or where they were born, has been touched by an angel and has infinite potential to develop psychically.

And remember, you were once a child and that child lives on in you. If for any reason your inner child is damaged or traumatised – not every childhood is a happy one – ask your angels to help you reconnect with that inner child. Close your eyes and visualise your adult self meeting that inner child. Tell that child you will never abandon them and that you will always love and protect them and be there whenever they cry.

ASKING FOR HELP

You may have noticed there is no set way to ask your angels for help, and that is deliberate. You don't have to go on bended knee, wait until a particular moon phase or consult your astrology charts; nor do you need to visit a healer or an angel expert to talk to your angels. You can do it anytime, anyplace and in your heart.

All of us talk to ourselves constantly. It's an ongoing conversation. All you need to do from now on is become aware of that self-talk, the questions you ask yourself, the things you tell yourself. Join in the conversation. It's been on autopilot and programmed by your ego for too long. Introduce your angel and let them upgrade. Let them steer the conversation to what is good and loving and kind. Listen to the other voices, but don't act on them. If these voices become harsh and unforgiving, imagine they are a cartoon character with a funny voice. They will soon lose their power.

When you feel in need of comfort and direction, just take a moment's silence and ask your angels to guide you. Then listen intently to what they have to say, through signs, in the coming days. It really is that simple.

You'll know when you are walking with angels when you notice:

- You're no longer taking things personally
- You don't feel a need to force your expectations on others
- You love to listen but also to ask questions
- You can't be anything but honest with your words
- You choose to do the next right thing
- Forgiveness is easy
- Gratitude is a theme
- Smiling feels natural to you
- You realise that you are enough
- Perhaps best of all, doing your best suddenly matters more to you than anything

When you notice all these things, angels are glowing within and all around you.

THEY SEE YOU

The enduring theme of this chapter – and indeed of this book – has been that angels can't be found outside yourself. They have to be awakened within *you*. And the simplest and fastest way to awaken your angels is to value yourself. Self-love is the doorway to revealing the truth about angels. When you nurture and respect yourself, the unseen energies of the universe reflect that loving care back to you.

You can be the kindest, most compassionate person in the world – an angel in the eyes of others – but if you don't love yourself, you won't see, hear and feel your angels. The universe treats you as you treat yourself.

And remember that your rituals – the things you actually choose to do every day – are far more powerful in spirit than your thoughts and feelings. In every moment your angels are watching what you do. They see you. Show them who you truly are. Notice your daily rituals. Notice how what you do makes you and those around you feel. Notice how positive actions raise you up and negative ones pull you down.

The more you repeatedly choose to do loving things for yourself and for others, the more your angels see you as their reflection on Earth. And the more like them you become, the more likely it is that you will be able to unleash your angel gene and the super-sensitive powers of empathy, compassion, intuition and kindness you were born to activate.

And all these sensitive superpowers culminate in the greatest gift and everyday miracle of them all – your dawning self-awareness that you can become an Earth angel. Every religion and belief system stresses the importance of knowing who you are, but nobody really explains why it matters or how to go about it. I hope this book has been your how-to guide to seeing the spiritual being – the aspiring angel – that you are truly born to be.

From now on you will no longer doubt your own potential or abilities, paranormal or otherwise, but will know exactly how to see, hear and feel angels – *start behaving like one*. And when you start behaving like the angel you were born to be, you'll finally discover your true meaning and purpose.

MAKING YOUR MARK

As this book draws to a close, I'm going to return to the search for objective truth, the science of angelic experiences referenced in Chapter Two that inspired it. Now I want to bring your attention back to your own biology – the science of you.

As well as an angel gene[78] – a gene that predisposes you towards mystic experiences or a sense that something unseen and greater than yourself is defining you – angelic traits, such as empathy and kindness, are also in your DNA. Remember, these sensitive traits have survived evolution because if we take care of each other we tend to thrive. How much you activate your inner angel is entirely up to you. But it's all there inside you – waiting. And it's waiting for a very important reason.

Empathy is an invisible inner sensing or understanding of another person's situation or point of view, seeing their heart and state of mind clearly. There is nothing more validating than to be seen or noticed. Studies[79] show that empathy has transformative benefits. It can foster a sense of connection with others, resolve conflict and ignite kindness in yourself and others. Kindness is another everyday angel miracle. When you are kind, feel-good hormones[80] are released, so the kinder you are the more likely you are to feel good, enjoy good health and even look younger (like natural Botox, being kind reduces the free-radical damage that ages you.[81]) Indeed, numerous studies[82] have confirmed that being a compassionate, kind person is a key to a beautiful life.

Another thing you may not know is that the more acts of kindness you perform, the more the areas of your brain associated with empathy are stimulated.[83] Just as muscles need a workout to stay toned, so too does your brain. If you are constantly negative, the areas of your brain associated with stress are strong, but if you choose to practise kindness, those stress areas get weaker and your kindness areas, or as I like to call them 'angel muscles', get stronger. And, as if all this wasn't enough, there is a 'pay it forward' effect; research shows that those who benefit from your kindness (as well as those who are third parties and just witness or find out about it) are inspired[84] to be kinder, changing the world for the better one angelic act at a time.

ON PURPOSE

So, if you feel your life lacks meaning and purpose, you need never feel that way again. A better world really can start with you and the next kind thing you choose to do. Every time you are kind or learn from your mistakes (we all make them), see yourself and others with eyes of compassion, strive to do your best or speak and act with integrity and humility, you are behaving like an angel and that has a ripple effect. You are bringing angels right down to Earth where they belong.

This isn't New or Now Age mumbo-jumbo. It's science. It's fact. Knowing that you already have within you what is needed to help heal the world and make it a better place because of the loving person you are is spiritual awakening and growth. There's no higher calling, no greater purpose, no better path to finding inner peace and your angels than that.

You finally understand that seeing angels 'out there' in the world around you, sensing there is something greater than yourself watching over you, and feeling from the inside out that your life is one of inner peace and purpose are all one and the same. Your outer and inner worlds merge. Truth and angels become one. There is no separation, just connection, angels within you and in everyone and everything.

I'll finish by letting you ponder the truth and power of this modern angel blessing:

Angels around us, angels beside us, angels within us.
Angels are watching over you when times are good or stressed.
Their wings wrap gently around you,
Whispering you are loved and blessed.

CONCLUSION

And the Truth Is . . .

It's already here. It's current.

Everything in this book has been preparing you for this moment – your recognition of what can only be called your primary or essential truth.

Essential truth is more than an acknowledgement of facts. It is recognising that the only reality is now, what you are currently feeling and doing. And if you are feeling empathy and doing kind things for yourself and others, you are activating your angel gene and discovering the self-aware consciousness that you and angels are one thing. There is no separation.

There is no separation between truth and angels either. Two powerful words. The former meaning 'what is' and the latter meaning 'what if'. And the truth about 'what if' can be found in the power of 'what is', which is the present – what you choose to feel and do right now.

There is absolutely nothing stopping you from becoming the angel you were born to be. The truth about angels is so very simple: you can see and become them now.

An angel is born every moment. Let the next one be you.

WINGING IT

Like anything that is precious or valuable, to help you unlock this essential truth about angels there are keys or codes you need to enter or progress through. These spiritual codes are simple and natural and you were born with them already in your heart. It's just a matter of remembering and activating them, every single day.

Here they are, and you may wish to personalise them or the order in which they are shown.

- Become present
- Show gratitude
- Practise self-care
- Look within
- Cultivate self-awareness
- Ask questions
- Listen
- Notice
- Wonder
- Do the right thing
- Release expectations
- Forgive yourself and others
- Keep your word
- Be kind
- Ignite your intuition
- Decode your dreams
- Do your best
- See, hear, and feel your angels

- Expect the unexpected
- Wing it

All these essential stages of spiritual awakening overlap and merge. A causal loop is a physics term meaning a sequence of events in which one event causes another, which in turn seems to cause the first event. The loop has no real start or finish and never ends. Each stage offers you glimpses of the essential and infinite truth, which is that angels are alive within and around you in the power of now. And it all forms a circle, with the beginning the same at the end but 'knowing the place for the first time,' in the immortal words of T. S. Eliot.

Once you truly understand that angels are not out there in some distant realm or afterlife, but always alive within you, you understand that inner peace is now, a place on Earth. You don't need to activate your third eye, ascend, meditate for hours, consult Ascended Masters, meets spirit guides, purchase crystals or jump through assorted New Age hoops to see it. You can feel and experience it in the present just by looking at yourself and everyone and everything with loving angel eyes. And when you do that you will realise that everyone is winging it.

There is nothing more magical than this life. And the life in spirit that you are leading begins right now. Yesterday has melted away and tomorrow has yet to materialise, so the only way angels can call out to you is through right *now*. The only thing that is truly angelic and deserves your complete respect and attention is the magic of *the present moment*.

BEAT BY BEAT

The magic of the present moment lies in the magic of your heart, of being aware that it beats. All the answers are in your heart, and the more you view your life as one eternal present moment, the better you can hear the voice of your heart.

How does your heart speak to you? Through feelings, of course, but in the spirit of science that this book celebrates, also through the way it beats.

Recent research from the Institute of HeartMath[85] has revealed that when you experience feelings of love, peace, creativity and joy, your heart beats in a calm and gentle way. The term coined by HeartMath for this is 'heart coherence', and it is a state of existence when your body and mind are in perfect harmony. Feelings of fear and anger have the opposite effect. So, when you connect with your heart in the present moment and experience feelings of love, you are physically, mentally and spiritually at your peak. You are one with your angels.

Seize the now. Don't think you necessarily need to be doing big things. As this book has hopefully made clear, a fulfilling life is about a series of precious small miracles that fill your heart with joy. It is about laughter with loved ones or your pet. It is about the bliss of a sunset or the enchantment of a moonlit lake. It is a song, a dream, a comfortable chair or a double rainbow peeking through after the rain. It is about a smile and a hug. It is about walking beside a river, dancing in the rain, or going for a walk without any destination in mind. It is about the satisfaction of a job well done, doing the right thing, keeping your word and filling each day with memories that never die. It is about so many 'insignificant' things, but when you add them up, they give you wings to fly.

Don't worry that you will lose your way, because the heart is always focused towards the light. And you don't have to be upbeat or get things right all the time either; you can also connect with your heart through facing your fears and challenges. Remember many of those things we think we know about angels are myths – you don't need to be perfect or 'gifted' to know them, just curious and willing to learn and grow.

Simply listen to your inner angel calling out to you gently through each beat of your heart – the place where all the answers are found, and all the miracles lie.

No time like the present: Close your eyes right now, keep them closed until you hear your own heart beating and then open them. See love coming from everyone and everything, most especially yourself. Even if you see things that are sad or unfair, notice the love trying to break through. Shift your perception from one of *fear* to one of *love*. See the world with angel eyes of love. Imagine your life free of conflict, fear, judgement and upset. Imagine yourself happy and living your dreams. Imagine loving yourself just the way you are. You don't need to seek love, because your heart is love already. You only need to eliminate the barriers of fear that you have built against it.

I ask you to imagine all this because it is possible to choose bliss at any moment – bliss is simply opening your heart and seeing angels and the love that goes with them wherever you go. It is possible because others before you have chosen that return to love. Why not make that choice now, while your heart is still beating?

TALKING TO YOU

If all this sounds familiar or moves you in some deep way, it is because it is talking to the aspiring angel within you. The angel within you has always known that fulfilment can only be found in your heart and true magic is following your dreams, not your fears. It's the part of you that longs to break through the limitations of fear and shine bright.

I pray that what you have uncovered here about yourself is a source of inner strength and helps heal any wounds you have suffered over the years for feeling like an outsider or imposter. I pray that it opens your mind to your infinite potential and helps you recognise that your instinct to be honest, empathetic and kind isn't your weakness, but your greatest strength, your superpower. I pray that you recognise that you do have a purpose – a great and important destiny – and that purpose is to discover and connect with the aspiring angel within you, so that you can become an inspiration to others and help the planet heal with your peaceful understanding that everyone and everything is connected by the power of love.

Don't waste any more moments; your aspiring angel is waiting for you.

And don't ever forget that whenever you really want to know the essential truth about angels, whenever you want to see an angel on Earth or an everyday miracle, just look in the mirror and smile with eyes of true love.

'This is a subtle truth: whatever you love you are.'

RUMI

RESOURCES

KEY ORGANISATIONS AND WEBSITES

SCIENTIFIC AND PARANORMAL

The Institute of Noetic Sciences (IONS)

www.noetic.org

Science-based, non-profit research, education and membership organisation dedicated to consciousness research and educational outreach, engaging a global learning community in the realisation of human potential.

Noetic.org/theresa-cheung/

This link takes you to a page specially created by IONS for Theresa Cheung readers. There are three wonderful free gifts from their research library waiting for you to download there.

The Windbridge Research Center

www.windbridge.org

Independent research organisation consisting of scientists and specialists researching mediumship and the paranormal. If you wish to book online readings with reasonably priced scientifically endorsed and ethical mediums, this is the place to visit.

Academy for the Advancement of Postmaterialist Sciences
www.aapsglobal.com
Promotes open-minded evidence-based enquiry into postmaterialist consciousness research.

The Parapsychological Association
www.parapsych.org
International professional organisation of scientists and scholars engaged in the scientific study of PSI (psychic) experiences.

The Rhine Research Center
www.rhine.org
Advances the science of parapsychology, provides education and resources for the public and fosters a community for individuals with personal and professional interest in PSI.

Forever Family Foundation
www.foreverfamilyfoundation.org
Furthers the understanding of Afterlife Science through research and education, while providing support and healing for people in grief.

The HeartMath Institute
www.heartmath.org
Provides free education and training programmes, services, research membership, and tools and technology to transform

people's lives by deepening their connection with their own hearts and the hearts of others for a peaceful future.

Association for the Scientific Study of Anomalous Phenomena
www.assap.ac.uk
Charity and learned society founded in 1981 to investigate, research and educate on a wide range of anomalous phenomena. Also carries out paranormal investigations and trains members to become accredited investigators.

Koestler Parapsychology Unit (KPU)
www.koestler-parapsychology.psy.ed.ac.uk
Research group based in the Psychology Department of the University of Edinburgh. Established in 1985, it consists of academics who teach and research various aspects of parapsychology.

Callum E. Cooper
www.callumecooper.com
Parapsychologist and author of *Telephone Calls from the Dead*, based at the University of Northampton: Centre for the Study of Anomalous Psychological Processes.

The Arthur Findlay College
www.arthurfindlaycollege.org
This psychic training college offers advice, courses, talks, information and training for potential mediums.

The College of Psychic Studies
www.collegeofpsychicstudies.co.uk
An educational charity offering regular classes, workshops, lectures and consultations in the field of psychic development.

The Galileo Commision
www.galileocommission.org
The Galileo Commission's remit is to open public discourse and to find ways to expand science so that it can accommodate and explore important human experiences and questions that science, in its present form, is unable to integrate.

The Premonition Code
www.thepremonitioncode.com
Website dedicated to *The Premonition Code* by neuroscientist Dr Julia Mossbridge and myself, where you can access free online lectures and scientifically endorsed precognition training.

Society of Psychical Research
www.spr.ac.uk
Founded in 1882 to conduct scholarly research into human experiences that challenge contemporary scientific models.

Society for Scientific Exploration
www.scientificexploration.org
A forum for sharing research into conventional and unconventional topics that cross mainstream boundaries and have profound implications for human knowledge and technology.

BEREAVEMENT AND CRISIS SUPPORT

Cruse Bereavement Care

www.cruse.org.uk

Not in any way connected to spirituality or research into the afterlife but a nationwide charity that exists to promote the well-being of bereaved people and to help anyone suffering a bereavement to understand their grief and cope with their loss. Offers confidential counselling and support, and advice about practical matters.

Bereavement Advice Centre

www.bereavementadvice.org

Free UK helpline, which gives practical information and advice on the many issues that face us after someone dies.

GriefShare

www.griefshare.org

US-based online support group and advice centre.

My Grief Angels

www.mygriefangels.org

Comprehensive list of links to resources and groups to help cope with the grieving process. The resources are organised by type of loss and there is a section on international resources, which is by country.

Helplines

UK: Samaritans 116 123

US: Crisis helpline 1-800-273-8255

FURTHER READING AND BIBLIOGRAPHY

SELECT BIBLIOGRAPHY

Alexander, E. *Proof of Heaven: A Neurosurgeon's Journey into the Afterlife*, Piatkus, 2016

Auerbach, L. *Psychic Dreaming*, Llewellyn, 2017

Coelho, P. *The Alchemist*, HarperCollins, 1995

Carter, C. *Science and the Near-death Experience: How Consciousness Survives Death*, Inner Traditions International, 2010

Cheung, T. *The Dream Dictionary A to Z*, HarperCollins, 2019

Cheung, T. *The Encyclopedia of Birthdays*, HarperCollins, 2020

Cheung, T. *The Dream Decoder Pack and Journal*, Laurence King, 2019

Cheung, T. *The Sensitive Soul,* Thread, 2019

Cheung, T. and Mossbridge, J. *The Premonition Code*, Watkins, 2017

Cheung, T. *The Afterlife Is Real*, Simon & Schuster, 2015

Cheung, T. and B *Answers from Heaven*, Piatkus, 2016

Cheung, T. *21 Rituals to Change Your Life*, Watkins, 2017

Cooper, Callum E. *Telephone Calls from the Dead*, Tricorn, 2012

Dossey, L. *One Mind: How Our Individual Mind Is Part of a Greater Consciousness and Why It Matters*, Hay House, 2014

Frankl, V. *Man's Search for Meaning*, Rider, 2004

Freke, T. *Soul Story: Evolution and the Purpose of Life*, Watkins, 2017

Keane L. *Surviving Death: A journalist investigates evidence for an afterlife,* Three Rivers Press, 2018

Kubler-Ross, E. *On Life After Death*, Celestial Arts, 2008

Kubler-Ross, E. and Kessler, D. *On Grief and Grieving*: Simon & Schuster, 2014

Mackesy, C. *The Boy, The Mole, The Fox and the Horse*, Ebury, 2019

Moody, R. (1975) *Life After Life*, Harper, 2015

Peck, M. S. *The Road Less Travelled*, Rider, 2020

Redfield, J. *The Celestine Prophecy*, Bantam, 1994

Sheldrake, R. *The Sense of Being Stared at and Other Aspects of the Extended Mind*, Cornerstone, 2013

Radin, D. *Real Magic*, Penguin, 2018

Radin, D. *Supernormal: Science, Yoga, and the Evidence for Extraordinary Psychic Abilities*, Deepak Chopra Press, 2013

Ruiz, D. M. *The Four Agreements*, Amber Allen, 2018

Tolle, E. *The Power of Now*, Yellow Kite, 2020

SPECIALIST

Do also refer to the endnotes.

Beischel, J. et al (2015) 'Anomalous information reception by research mediums under blinded conditions II: Replication and extension.' *EXPLORE: The Journal of Science & Healing*, 11(2), 136–142. doi: 10.1016/j.explore.2015.01.001

Beischel, J. et al (2014–2015) 'The possible effects on bereavement of assisted after-death communication during readings with psychic mediums: a continuing bonds perspective.' *Omega: Journal of Death and Dying*, 70(2), 169–194. doi: 10.2190/OM.70.2b

Beischel, J. *Among Mediums: A Scientist's Quest for Answers*, Windbridge, 2013

Beischel, J. *Investigating Mediums*, Windbridge, 2016

Beischel, J. and Schwartz, G. (2007) 'Anomalous information reception by research mediums demonstrated using a novel triple-blind protocol.'

Bem, D. et al (2015) 'Feeling the future: a meta-analysis of 90 experiments on the anomalous anticipation of random future events.' *Pub Med*, 2, 2015, 30 Oct, 4:1188

Baruss, I. and Mossbridge, J. *Transcendent Mind: Rethinking the Science of Consciousness,* American Psychological Association, 2016

Facco, E. and Agrillo, C. (2012) 'Near-death experiences between science and prejudice'. *Frontiers in Human Neuroscience*, 2012, 18 July

Fenwick, E. and Fenwick, P. *The Truth in the Light: An Investigation of over 300 NDEs*, White Crow Books, 2012

Greyson, B. (2010) 'Seeing dead people not known to have died: "Peak in Darien" experiences.' *Anthropology and Humanism*, 2010, November, 35(2) 159–71

Kelly, E. W. and Arcangel, D. (2011) 'An investigation of mediums who claim to give information about deceased persons.' *Journal of Nervous and Mental Disease*, 2011, Jan: 199(1) 11–7

May, E. et al *The Stargate Archives*, McFarland Jefferson, 2017

May, E. et al *Extrasensory Perception: Support, skepticism and science*, Praeger, 2015

Mossbridge, J. et al (2012) 'Predictive physiological anticipation preceding seemingly unpredictable stimuli: a meta-analysis.' *IONS*

Nahm, M. et al (2011) 'Terminal lucidity: A review and a case collection.' *Archives of Gerontology and Geriatrics*, 2012, Jul 55(1) 138–42

Nelson, R. and Bancel, P. (2011) 'Effects of mass consciousness: changes in random data during global events.' *Explore*, NY, Nov–Dec 2011, 7(6) 373–83

Parnia, S. et al (2014) 'Awareness during resuscitation – a prospective study.' *Resuscitation, Dec 2014*, 85(12), 1799–1805

Radin, D. I. (2011) 'Predicting the unpredictable: 75 years of experimental evidence.' IONS

Radin, D. I. and Schlitz, M. J. (2005) 'Gut feelings, intuition, and emotions: an exploratory study.' *The Journal of Alternative and Complementary Medicine*, 2005, 11(1) 85–91

Schmidt, S. (2012) 'Can we help just by good intentions? A meta-analysis of experiments on distant intention effects.' *Journal of Alternative and Complementary Medicine*, 2012, June 18 (6) 529–33

Targ, R. *The Reality of ESP: A Physicist's Proof of Psychic Abilities*, Quest, 2012

Tart, C. *The End of Materialism: How Evidence of the Paranormal Is Bringing Science and Spirit Together*, New Harbinger, 2009

Townsend, R. *Hero, Hawk and Open Hand*, Yale University Press, 2004

Van Lommel, P. et al (2013) 'Non-local consciousness: A concept based on scientific research on near-death experiences during cardiac arrest.' *Journal of Consciousness Studies*, 2013, 20, 7–48

ANGEL TERMINOLOGY

You will probably encounter a huge number of tempting angel therapies, products, courses and teaching systems. Below I'm going to briefly run through some of the terminology you are likely to come across and suggest some pros and cons. I want to stress that I am expressing my opinion here and not fact. If any healer or method helps you feel closer to your angels, go ahead. But be very cautious and think before you part with any hard-earned cash, or place your trust in someone or something.

The list below is brief by design and references spiritual terminology and associations not yet used in the book.

Akashic Records

The term for this in Jungian psychology is the 'collective unconscious'; it is where shared information, or information that is innate, is stored. Akashic records is the term more commonly used in spiritual/lightworker/angel contexts. It refers to a non-physical, energetic, vibrational record of everything that has ever happened to every soul that has ever existed. Some psychics claim to be able to read your soul record. Whether or not that is true can't be proved and is a matter of personal trust and belief.

Alchemy

In medieval times this was the term for transforming metal into gold but, in spiritual terms, it refers to working towards your highest and purest self, discovering the aspiring angel within you. In other words, angel alchemy is everything this book is about.

Angel Cards

Some lightworkers prefer to channel messages from angels using cards. There are different types of angel deck cards – for example, oracle, Tarot and healing – but they are all used for giving readings. Some card decks are said to reveal which angel is sending you a message. As a former Tarot card reader, I know that card decks can help trigger associations and are great tools[86] for self-understanding, as they are all based on archetypes or collective human experiences. But I don't believe they have any power in themselves. The power is *you*.

As an aside, you may come across places where lightworkers or psychics do live card readings online for their followers. Beyond helping you to understand the meanings of certain cards and it all being rather entertaining, there's little value in this. And if you see someone shuffling their cards offscreen, chances are they have pre-picked them. It's not to be taken seriously, especially if a crystal ball is introduced into the mix.

Angel Healing/Therapy/Reiki

Angel healing is an alternative healing and therapy concept that encourages you to connect to your angels. It is typically heavily structured around angel hierarchies and involves a lightworker designing a course you can follow in which they act as mentor and guide, connecting you to specific angels.

If it helps you feel better about yourself and your life, connects you to like-minded sensitive souls and you can afford the time and money, this may be the angel path for you. However, to risk repeating myself, the most powerful way to connect to your angels and to experience their healing is to find out about angels yourself and connect to them in your own unique way. And whatever you decide to do, avoid becoming dependent on a course or a particular lightworker, however much you admire them or however connected to a higher vibration they claim to be.

Angel reiki is typically done via a channel or psychic who tunes into their intuition and gently places their hands on or near your body. There is no massage involved. Sometimes the healing is done with the healer's thoughts rather than in person. The idea is that the channel helps release blocks to your spiritual energy. It's reiki healing – which is energy healing – with angels tagged on. Some doctors recommend energy healing for its therapeutic benefits and some studies do report promising results.

Archangel Healing

In my opinion, angels don't organise themselves according to a hierarchy and I don't understand why angel healing isn't enough and there have to be archangels – as if that's somehow better – or, for that matter, female and male archangels. It's a very human way of thinking about angels – but we *are* human beings, so it is understandable. A way to look at it is that by 'breaking down' angels like this we can perhaps better understand the angels' holistic nature.

Animal Guide/Totem

This is a symbol that serves as a spirit guide to help you get in touch with the specific qualities of that animal, which may be traits you need to nurture or deal with. You can call on your animal totem during times of stress to give you what you need to cope. I'm an animal lover, so anything that brings people closer to animals is progress, in my opinion.

Astral Plane

This is the term used for levels of consciousness that lie beyond the material. There are said to be numerous astral planes and levels, and some channels claim to be able tell you all about them because they regularly travel to them. Whether this is true or not, maybe it can help you by reminding you of your own psychic potential.

Astrology

This is the art of charting the positions of the planets and stars when you were born and the signs of the zodiac that are contained among them. I believe the 'as above, so below' theory has some weight and scientific evidence to back it up. We all know the moon rules the tides and we humans are made up of up to 70 per cent water, so it's logical. Astrology is a wonderful self-help tool[87] that can help you understand yourself and others. Angel astrology is simply connecting certain angels with the signs of the zodiac to emphasise the qualities of that sign and advise on the best spiritual path. In short, it's astrology with spiritual wisdom added into the mix!

Aura

This is the invisible energy field thought to surround every living being. People who are psychic claim to be able to see auras, shaped like a giant egg, around each person. The aura can tell a psychic about a person's personality, health and spiritual development. In my opinion, rather than you trusting someone else's vision/understanding of yourself, your angels would prefer you to create and develop your own.

It is said that there are seven colours of the rainbow in each aura and that every person has a dominant aura colour, but the colours constantly change. Sounds like colour therapy by another name to me! I'm a big fan of colour therapy to boost mood, as research shows that the colours we wear and surround ourselves with can have an impact – positive and negative – on our moods. For example, red symbolises creativity and vitality, so wear red if you need a dose of courage. Yellow represents intelligence and confidence. Blue is the colour of peace, green of harmony, white the colour of purity and so on. Purple is all about spiritual awakening, so I hope you are wearing lots of that!

Chakras

These are energy centres believed to be located at various points on our bodies, with each chakra being associated with a certain quality. For example, the crown chakra, located at the top of the head, is associated with higher awareness. If this approach speaks to you, I encourage you to research and meditate on your chakras. Remember, though, that meditation isn't the complicated art it is often presented as. Every time you are fully absorbed and paying such close attention that you lose all track of time, you are meditating. I hope reading this book is having that effect!

Crystals and Essential Oils

Certain crystals are believed to carry energy that can comfort, heal and inspire. It makes sense to me as crystals come from the earth. There is also some scientific evidence to suggest they may have subtle healing powers. My favourite angel crystal is rose quartz, as it is associated with unconditional love.

Essential oils are similar. There is some, but not enough, scientific evidence to prove their efficacy, and plenty of anecdotal evidence from those who swear by them. My favourite angel essential oils are clary sage, angelica seed and frankincense, but I encourage you to do your own research and find out which aroma is most like an angel kiss to you.

Numerology

Numerology is similar to astrology in that it suggests the universe has a system; but, instead of that system being in the stars, it is based on numbers. Understanding the numbers in your life – from the day you were born to your house or phone number – can help you understand yourself and the world around you better. Angel numerology is the idea that angels can communicate their wisdom to you through numbers or a combination of numbers. One of the most powerful angel numbers or signs is believed to be 11 (see page 157), but every number contains a message from your angels. Numerology is utterly fascinating,[88] and I encourage you to notice the power of the numbers in your life and find out more. Angel numerology is simply numerology with the focus placed on your spiritual growth.

Reincarnation

Reincarnation – the idea that your spirit has had previous lives and will have future lives – is a compelling one that also makes a lot of sense; maybe it explains why bad things happen to good people. Past-life therapy,[89] where hypnosis is sometimes used to uncover memories of past lives, is believed to be healing. Anything that helps you understand yourself better is positive, in my opinion, and there is some promising research out there about reincarnation (see page 38). However, I strongly feel that when it comes to your spiritual growth, the power is *now*. This life is where your focus needs to be, rather than getting wrapped up in the drama of previous (or future) lives.

Spirit Guides

These are supposedly the spirits of Ascended Masters who have passed on and attained a high level of wisdom but have chosen to remain close to Earth to guide certain individuals. You may also hear terms like the Wise Council of Elders; they are there to support you and help your spiritual growth or even choose your next life. Apparently, there is a whole afterlife network; the more I learn about this, the more I think it sounds like a spiritual version of LinkedIn. If believing all this to be true of the afterlife helps you feel loved and protected from above, so be it.

Spiritual Advisor

This term refers to anyone with an understanding of spirituality, who can empathetically and intuitively sense the optimal way for you to overcome spiritual blocks. In other words, a wise soul (shaman, psychic, healer, medium, lightworker) who may be able to offer you essential life wisdom. We all need guidance from time to time and to feel loved and protected, so there's no harm in consulting one as long as you remain cautious.

GUIDELINES FOR VISITING MEDIUMS AND LIGHTWORKERS

These guidelines apply to mediums, psychics, angel experts, energy healers and all lightworkers.

A word on terminology: there is a difference between a medium and a psychic; a medium connects to the afterlife and spirit guides, whereas a psychic can sense things about you in the present. However, many mediums are also psychics and some psychics have mediumistic gifts, so there is crossover.

Additionally, a channel receives information from the unseen realm, and angel healers work with energy to offer you healing.

All fall into the category of lightworkers because they are connecting to the unseen force of goodness, love and light on your (and the world's) behalf.

Are they qualified?

The Windbridge Research Center tests mediums scientifically. The lead researcher there, Dr Julie Beischel, gave up a potentially lucrative career in the pharmaceutical industry following a visit to a medium who revealed with astonishing accuracy the circumstances of her mother's death. Dr Beischel wondered what would happen if mediums were tested in the same rigorous way that drugs were. Her research at the Windbridge Research Center is raising scientific eyebrows;[90] it centres on volunteer mediums working in conditions where all possibility of cold reading (picking up clues from the client) is removed. To become a Windbridge-certified medium takes years of testing and study. Few qualify. Those who do are listed on the Center's website. (Note:

Windbridge, along with IONS, is also pioneering research[91] into the genetic traits of mediums and psychics).

If a medium is not certified in this way, look at their background. There are mediumship programmes run by fine establishments, like the Arthur Findlay College in the UK. If a medium's training background is non-existent or obscure or celebrity-endorsed, avoid them; and be equally wary of anyone who seems to have an almost cult-like following. Watch out, too, for a worrying trend towards spiritual narcissism.[92]

Other than that, it is in the end a matter of trusting your gut. Some fine mediums have worked humbly and quietly for years in local churches and at psychic fairs; you may strike lucky and find an authentic one. Experiment by all means, but **not** when you feel vulnerable. Put your sceptic's hat on. Ask questions. Don't believe everything you are told and remember the old adage: if something sounds too good to be true, it is.

Do they charge huge fees?

If they do, avoid them. Some people say that mediums should not charge at all for their services, but this doesn't make sense; of course you should pay. You are paying for a service from someone who hopefully has training and certainly has experience. But the fees should be no more than what you would pay for a good haircut.

Is there branding and marketing surrounding their work? Do they have a book, show or course to sell?

Their books or courses may be worth checking out, as some do offer precious wisdom, but, generally, if there is a lot of attention surrounding a medium, it is more likely that they're concerned with making themselves a spiritual celebrity, not with helping you or anyone else.

Ethics

An honest medium will have a code of ethics. They should only need to see you once, or certainly no more than three times. If they can't offer proof of spirit survival, they should offer to refund any fees. If they pressure you to make repeat visits, avoid them. This could easily lead to dependency.

Do they make you feel good about yourself?

Mediums aren't therapists or entertainers, but if they can make true contact with the afterlife you should notice a lightness, a joyful energy about them. If they are overly serious and intense, avoid them. And you should also feel empowered by their message, and more confident about yourself and your own ability to make the right decisions.

Do they 'know' what you need to do?

If a medium tells you exactly what decision you should make, this is dangerous territory. The only person qualified to make decisions about your life is you. They can offer suggestions, but no more than that.

Do they do video or phone readings or insist on meeting in person?

Some mediums prefer to work in person, but it is a myth that you need to be there in person for a reading. The most promising research on mediums so far (see page 34) was done via the phone, to eliminate all possibility of cold reading. If you are not comfortable meeting a medium, the genuine ones should be able to offer you readings via video call or over the phone. But be aware that psychic phone lines and services are best avoided because they do not typically have qualified mediums or psychics working for them.

Note: There are a number of ongoing studies focusing on identifying common traits among mediums and psychics. Typically these studies suggest psychic ability appears to run in families, has a genetic component, but other unusual factors, such as being left handed or experience of childhood traumas or autoimmune disorders are also being identified.

YOUR FREE GIFTS

Subscribe to my free monthly newsletter for free gifts, readers' stories, updates and more via my website
www.theresacheung.com

You can also listen to all episodes of my *White Shores* podcast – the podcast for spiritual beings having a human experience – at this link:
www.buzzsprout.com/361061

Season 1 can be found on the podcast page of my website www.theresacheung.com and all seasons can be found wherever you download your podcasts. *White Shores* features interviews with some of the world's leading scientists researching the paranormal, honest mediums and lightworkers, true-life stories, expert insight, rituals, dream interpretation, laughter and more. I'd be honoured and grateful if you could leave a review, as it helps spread the word that 'spiritual is real'.

And if you message me at angeltalk710@aol.com with your reflections on this book and/or what angels mean to you I will reply in due course and send you a free angel attracting gift.

CALLING ALL ANGELS: HOW TO CONTACT THE AUTHOR

If you have a question, story or insight, please don't hesitate to get in touch with me.

You can contact me via: angeltalk710@aol.com. You could also message me via my author pages on Facebook, Instagram and Twitter. I aim to reply to everyone in due course. Don't feel alone in your quest for truth and your angels, or that anything you have to say is not important enough. I welcome and value all your thoughts, questions and stories. Communicating with you is the thing I love most about writing spiritual books.

ACKNOWLEDGEMENTS

Deep gratitude to my editor Carolyn Thorne for her clear guidance, understanding and vision. Thanks also to Jacqui Lewis for her magnificent (and much-needed) copy-edit, to Holly Whitaker for making sure everything was pulled together on time, to Myrto Kalavrezou for her publicity inspiration, and to everyone at Yellow Kite, Hodder & Stoughton involved in the production and promotion of this book. I am especially indebted to Ingrid Court-Jones for her truly invaluable input while writing and editing this book.

The Truth About Angels would not have felt complete without the voices of the extraordinary people who generously gave me permission to share their true-life experiences here. I can't thank them enough as they are the voices of Earth angels. I sincerely hope their contribution will encourage other sensitive souls to share their stories and spread the truth about angels to help heal the world.

Gratitude also to the scientists and experts out there researching consciousness, in particular the inspirational Dr Helané

Wahbeh and her brilliant science team led by the extraordinary pioneer, Dr Dean Radin, and to the visionary Dr Julia Mossbridge. I'd also like to thank every guest who has appeared on my *White Shores* podcast – your interviews are all heartfelt and have become talking points.

Sincere thanks to my infinitely wise agent Jane Graham Maw (www.grahammawchristie.com) for her patience and belief. I am also forever in debt to my amazing readers, who are a constant source of inspiration to me. Thank you to Matthew for running my social media and taking care of all the technical stuff for me with such creative flair and to my son, Robert for brilliantly producing and editing *White Shores*. Last, but never least, heartfelt thanks to the true angels in my life: Ray, Robert, Ruthie (and my little dog, Arnie) for their love and support, as I went into self-imposed exile to declare my truth in this book.

ABOUT THE AUTHOR

Theresa Cheung has been researching and writing about angels, dreams, and personal and spiritual growth for the past twenty-five years. She has an MA from King's College, University of Cambridge in Theology and English and is the author of many internationally bestselling books, including two *Sunday Times* Top-10 angel bestsellers. Her book *The Dream Dictionary from A to Z* (HarperCollins) is regarded as a classic in its field, regularly bouncing to Amazon's number 1 in its category. Her spiritual books have been translated into more than forty languages and she has written many features for national newspapers and magazines. Her media appearances include an interview with Piers Morgan on *GMTV*, Episode 71 of Russell Brand's *Under the Skin* podcast, BBC Radio 4 and Five Live, decoding dreams live on Coast to Coast AM, Channel 4, and the *Today* morning show in Australia. She has conducted dream decoding webinars for leading brands such as Beauty Bay, Dusk and Anthropologie and works closely with scientists studying consciousness. She has her own popular spiritual podcast, *White Shores*. Her website is www.theresacheung.com and she has a busy author page on Facebook, as well as pages on Instagram and Twitter.

'Speak your truth quietly and clearly.'

DESIDERATA

ENDNOTES

1 Silveira, L. 'Experimenting with Spirituality: Analyzing *The God Gene* in a Nonmajors Laboratory Course' *CBE Life Sci Education,* 2008 Spring; 7(1): 132–145

2 Heathcote James, E. (2009) *Seeing Angels – True Contemporary Accounts of Hundreds of Angelic Experiences*, John Blake, 2009

3 Episode 3, Season 1, *White Shores* and Episode 16, Season 2, *White Shores*

4 Parnia, S. 'Death and consciousness – an overview of the mental and cognitive experience of death'. *Annals of the New York Academy of Sciences*, November 2014, 1330, 75–93

5 Beischel, J. et al 'Anomalous information reception by research mediums under blinded conditions II: replication and extension' *Explore* (NY) Mar–Apr 2015,11(2),136–42. doi: 10.1016/j.explore.2015.01.001. Epub 2015 Jan 7.

6 Episode 10, Season 1, *White Shores*

7 Episode 4, Season 1, *White Shores*

8 Episode 8, Season 1, *White Shores*

9 Episode 11, Season 1, *White Shores*

10 Episode 11, Season 1, *White Shores*

11 https://noetic.org/science/research

12 www.edgarcayce.org

13 https://historycollection.com/project-stargate-10-facts-about-the-us-government-psychic-experiments

14 Wahbeh, H. et al (2018) 'A mixed methods phenomenological and exploratory study of channelling' *Journal of the Society for Psychical Research* 82(3) 129–148; Wahbeh, H. et al 'Exceptional experiences reported by scientists and engineers' *Explore* 14(5) 329–341

15 Mossbridge, J. et al (2012) 'Predictive physiological anticipation preceding seemingly unpredictable stimuli: a meta-analysis'. *Frontiers in Psychology*, 3(390)

16 https://atwar.blogs.nytimes.com/2012/03/27/navy-program-to-study-how-troops-use-intuition

17 Radin, D. *Supernormal*, Random House, 2013

18 Bem D. et al (2016) 'Feeling the future: A meta-analysis of 90 experiments on the anomalous anticipation of random future events' *F10000Research*, 4(1188)

19 Utts, J. (2016) 'Appreciating Statistics' *Journal of the American Statistical Association*, 111(516) 1373–1380; https://psi-encyclopedia.spr.ac.uk/articles/jessica-utts

20 Tressoldi, P. et al (2011) 'Extraordinary claims require extraordinary evidence: a classical and Bayesian review of evidences, *Frontiers in Psychology*, 2(117); Williams, B. J. (2011) 'Revisiting the ganzfeld ESP debate: A basic review and assessment' *Journal of Scientific Exploration*, 25(4) 639–661

21 Sheldrake, R. *Dogs That Know When Their Owners Are Coming Home and Other Unexplained Powers of Animals*, Crown, 1999

22 Lipton, B. *The Biology of Belief*, Hay House, 2015

23 Bosch, H. et al 'Examining psychokinesis: The interaction of human intention with random number generators – a meta-analysis' *Psychological Bulletin*, July 2006, 132(4), 497–523

24 Nelson, R. et al 'Correlations of continuous random data with major world events' *Foundations of Physics Letters,* December 2002, 15(6), 537–550

25 https://noetic.org/blog/phase-1-energy-healing-study-success

26 Schmidt, S. (2012) 'Can we help just by good intentions? A meta-analysis of experiments on distant intention effects' *Journal of Alternative and Complementary Medicine*, 18(6), 529–533

27 Mossbridge, J. et al *Transcendent Mind, Rethinking the Science of Consciousness*, American Psychological Association, 2016

28 https://med.virginia.edu/perceptual-studies/who-we-are/dr-ian-stevenson

29 https://galileocommission.org/report

30 https://www.thesoulphonefoundation.org Episode 11, Season 2, *White Shores*

31 An interesting aside is that IONS, and the noetic research undertaken there, feature in Dan Brown's novel *The Last Symbol*. In fact, the motivation of the lead character is based on what Dan Brown learned from the time he spent investigating the experiments conducted at IONS.

32 Polls also show that while belief in God has declined in recent years belief in an afterlife has steadily increased: https://www.nbcnews.com/better/wellness/fewer-americans-believe-god-yet-they-still-believe-afterlife-n542966

33 dailymail.co.uk/femail/article-5129875/women-believe-prove-theres-life-death.html

34 Episode 50, *Be Reasonable*; Merseyside Skeptics Society podcast with Michael Marshall.

35 Knight, F. (2021) *Good Grief: The A to Z Approach of Modern-day Grief Healing*, O Books.

36 Neal, D. et al 'How do people adhere to goals when willpower is low? The profits and pitfalls of strong Habits'. *American Journal of Personality and Social Psychology*, Jun 2013; 104(6): 959–75: doi 10.1037/a0032626 Hobson, N. M. et al 'Rituals decrease the neural response to performance failure'. 2017; *PeerJ*, e3363, doi: 10.7717/peerj.3363 Brooks, A. et al 'Don't Stop Believing: Rituals Improve Performance by Decreasing Anxiety'. Harvard Business School, Jan 2017: http://faculty.chicagobooth.edujane.risen/research/Don't_stop_believing_rituals.pdf 4 Norton, M. and Hino, F. 'Rituals alleviate grieving for loved ones, loves and lotteries'. *Journal of Experimental Psychology*, Feb 2014; 143(1): 266–72: doi:10.1037 a0031772. Epub 11 Feb 2013; Conman, A. 'Designing personal grief rituals: An analysis of symbolic objects and actions'. Lancaster University Research portal, *Death Studies*, 19 June 2016: www.research.lancs. ac.uk/portal/en/publications/designing-personal-griefrituals (6f440948-5f38-45aa-bad1-9573ecfad1c3).html

37 www.scientificamerican.com/article/why-ritualswork; www.bakadesuyo.com/2015/10/ritual/

38 Lally, P. 'How are habits formed: Modelling habit formation in the real world'. *European Journal of Social Psychology*, Oct 2010; 40(6): 998–1009

39 https://www.independent.co.uk/life-style/people-who-read-books-are-nicer-kingston-university-study-fiction-a7721096.html
40 https://www.wired.com/2011/01/the-neuroscience-of-music
41 https://greatergood.berkeley.edu/article/item/five_ways_mindfulness_meditation_is_good_for_your_health
42 https://www.youtube.com/watch?v=v-nptoFE1Js
43 Milán, E. G. 'Auras in mysticism and synaesthesia: A comparison'. *Consciousness and Cognition*, March 2012, 21(1), 258–268
44 www.sciencedaily.com/releases/2020/02/200225164210.htm
45 Lai, S. et al '"The Three Good Things" – The effects of gratitude practice on wellbeing: A randomised controlled trial' *Health Psychology*, March 2017, 26(1):10
46 Time.com/4737286/multitasking-mental-health-stress-texting-depression
47 www.scientificamerican.com/article/mental-downtime/
48 www.cam.ac.uk/cammagazine/benefitsofboredom
49 Fogli, A. et al 'Our dreams, our selves: automatic analysis of dream reports' *Royal Society of Open Science*, August 2020, royalsocietypublishing.org/doi/10.1098/rsos.192080
50 Einstein said his career was inspired by a dream in which he was riding a sledge and approaching the speed of light where all colours blended into one. The speed of light was the key to Einstein's theory of relativity.
51 Cooper, C. E. et al 'Anomalous experiences and the bereavement process' *Death, Dying, and Mysticism*, Thomas Cattoi and Christopher Moreman, 2015, 117–131
52 Episode 6, Season 2, *White Shores*
53 Check out vintage footage online of Christian the lion reunited with his owners. Listen to *White Shores*, Episodes 6 and 13, Season 2 and Episode 14, Season 3.
54 You can hear Louise tell the story in her own words in Episode 11, Season 3 of *White Shores*.
55 You can hear Kandy share this story in her own words in Episode 4, Season 3 of *White Shores*.
56 Also listen to Episode 1, Season 2, *White Shores*, in which I talk to bestselling author Tim Freke about spiritual awakening and the meaning of life discovered in our constant evolution.
57 Silveira, L. 'Experimenting with Spirituality: Analyzing *The God Gene* in a Nonmajors Laboratory Course' *CBE Life Sci Education*,

2008 Spring; 7(1), 132–145, www.ncbi.nlm.nih.gov/pmc/articles/PMC2262126

58 Aron, E. et al (2012) 'Sensory processing sensitivity: a review in the light of evolution of biological responsibility' *Personality and Social Psychology Review* 16(3), 262–284

59 Acevedo, B. et al 'The highly sensitive brain: an fMRI study of sensory processing sensitivity and response to others' emotions' *Brain and Behaviour*, July 2014, 4(4), (4) 580–594

60 Israel, S. et al (2009) 'The oxytocin receptor contributes to prosocial fun allocations in the dictator game and the social orientations task.' *PLOS ONE*, 4(5) e5535.

61 NDE research and debate is ongoing and I am eagerly following Dr Parnia's follow-up studies, as well as those of other pioneers, such as Dutch near-death experience researcher, Dr Pim van Lommel, who can find no medical explanation for NDEs. The belief that it is hallucination persists. Parapsychologist Dr Caroline Watts, who provocatively asserted in 2020 that NDEs are all in the brain, simply dismissed outright the possibility of a paranormal explanation. This is disappointing for a scientist as potential explanations should not be dismissed before even investigating them. Despite this, there is also every indication of a growing body of evidence suggesting the possibility of life after death as an explanation for NDEs.

62 As well as my interview with Dr Eben Alexander in Episode 1, Season 1 of my *White Shores* podcast you may also wish to listen to my interview with David Ditchfield, who 'died' on the train tracks but returned to share his astonishing near-death experience in Episode 9, Season 2 of *White Shores*. I also talk in Episode 12, Season 1 to Dr Penny Sartori, the leading expert on NDEs.

63 Although deathbed visions have been recorded since the beginning of time, one of the most noted scientific studies into these visions was carried out in the 1970s by Dr Karlis Osis for a book entitled *At the Hour of Death*, which considered thousands of studies and interviewed over a thousand doctors, nurses and relatives who attended the dying. Once again, the research uncovered a number of striking consistencies including:

- Whether or not a person believes in an afterlife is immaterial.
- Most people report seeing loved ones who have passed over.
- These loved ones in spirit often tell them that they are there to help them cross over.

- The dying person is typically reassured and comforted by these visions.
- The dying person's health is sometimes restored temporarily, or their pain is relieved momentarily by these visions.
- During the experience the dying person tends to be aware of their real surroundings and does not seem to be hallucinating.

64 Listen to Episode 18, Season 3 of *White Shores* with death doula Debra Diamond.

65 Episode 8, Season 3, *White Shores*

66 Episode 9, Season 1, *White Shores*

67 Episode 7, Season 1, *White Shores*

68 Episode 10, Season 1 White Shores with Dr Delorme

69 Delorme, A. et al 'Intuitive assessment of mortality based on facial characteristics' *Explore*, 14(4), 262–267

70 *Answers from Heaven*, Piatkus, 2017 and Episode 2, Season 1, *White Shores*

71 www.thepremonitioncode.com. Visit this site for scientifically endorsed precognitive testing and training offered by my *Premonition Code* co-author Dr Julia Mossbridge. Warning: it's tough going.

72 Episode 5, Season 1, *White Shores*

73 Theresa Cheung *An Angel Healed Me,* Simon & Schuster

74 Theresa Cheung *Ten Secrets of Heaven*, Simon & Schuster, 2015

75 www.webmd.com/balance/features/can-prayer-heal#1

76 Episode 2, Season 2, *White Shores*

77 Episode 2, Season 3, *White Shores*: The Real Vicar of Dibley

78 Hamer, D. *The God Gene: How faith is hard wired into our genes*, Doubleday, 2004.

79 Reiss, H. 'The Science of Empathy' *Journal of Patient Experience*, 2017, 4(2), 74–77; Otake, K. et al (2006) 'Happy people become happier through kindness: A counting kindnesses intervention' *Journal of Happiness Studies*, September 2006, 7(3), 361–375. Kindness boosts immunity. Research suggests that when people watch or perform acts of kindness themselves, antibodies in the immune system indicating immune-system health increase significantly. This impact of kindness has been called the Mother Teresa effect – a study showed that after students watched a film about the good deeds of Mother Teresa, their immune systems were strengthened.

80 Esch, T. et al (2011) 'The neurobiological link between compassion and love'. *Medical Science Monitor*, 17(3) RA65–RA75. Published online 2011 March.

81 Szeto, A. et al 'Oxytocin attenuates NADP-dependent superoxide activity and IL6 secretion in macrophages and vascular cells' *American Journal of Endocrinology and Metabolism*, December 2008, 295(6), E1495.

82 Lyubomirsky, S. et al (2004) 'Pursing sustained happiness through random acts of kindness and counting one's blessings: tests of two-week interventions', Department of Psychology, University of California, Riverside

83 Engström, M. and Söderfeldt, B. 'Brain activation during compassion meditation' *The Journal of Alternative and Complementary Medicine*, 2010, 16(5) 597–9

84 www.scientificamerican.com/article/kindness-contagion; Theresa Cheung *100 Ways to Be Kind*, Thread Books, 2020

85 www.heartmath.org

86 Episode 5, Season 2, *White Shores*

87 Theresa Cheung *The Encyclopaedia of Birthdays*, HarperCollins, 2020 and Episode 20, Season 2, *White Shores*

88 Episode 14, Season 2, *White Shores*

89 Episode 19, Season 2, *White Shores*

90 Beischel, J. et al 'Anomalous information reception by research mediums under blinded conditions II: replication and extension' *Explore* (NY) Mar–Apr 2015, 11(2),136–42

91 Psychics: IONS research suggests there may be a genetic component in psychic ability, the 'gift' handed down the generations noetic.org/research/genetics-of-psychic-ability. Mediums: Listen to Episode 2, Season 1, *White Shores* – the Windbridge Research Center study suggests that, although there are many exceptions, common traits or traits that feature more often than others among the mediums they have studied include being left-handed; being gay or lesbian; and having experience of childhood trauma.

92 Read: Derren Brown's book *Tricks of the Mind*.

books to help you live a good life

Join the conversation and tell
us how you live a #goodlife

@yellowkitebooks

YellowKiteBooks

Yellow Kite Books

YellowKiteBooks